The
Season

A blueprint for hockey coaches

Doug Ringrose

Order this book online at www.trafford.com
or email orders@trafford.com

Most Trafford titles are also available at major online book retailers.

Note for Librarians: A cataloguing record for this book is available from Library
and Archives Canada at www.collectionscanada.ca/amicus/index-e.html

Printed in Victoria, BC, Canada.

ISBN:978-1-4251-8190-1 (SC)

*Our mission is to efficiently provide the world's finest, most comprehensive book publishing
service, enabling every author to experience success. To find out how to publish your book, your
way, and have it available worldwide, visit us online at www.trafford.com*

Trafford rev. 8/26/2009

 www.trafford.com

North America & international
toll-free: 1 888 232 4444 (USA & Canada)
phone: 250 383 6864 ♦ fax: 812 355 4082

Introduction

I'm just an ordinary Canadian guy. I grew up playing minor hockey in Edmonton, Alberta and I did go on to play some junior hockey. After I finished playing, I got involved in coaching and had a couple of very enjoyable years at it before life became too busy. I had to set different priorities for a while and I concentrated on my education and establishing career. Establishing a family was next on the agenda. My wife Lorraine and I had three sons and once they arrived time became even more limited. I still loved watching the game of hockey but I really didn't foresee much more participation.

What lured me back to the game was the interest that my oldest son Michael was developing at a very early age. He was born in Edmonton just prior to the Edmonton Oilers great run of five Stanley Cups in seven seasons. The city was always abuzz with hockey excitement and we spent many enjoyable evenings watching games on TV and, as he grew older, attending some live games at what used to be called "The Coliseum."

Mike was a big fan of Grant Fuhr and his original aspiration was to be a goaltender. We registered him in hockey and always encouraged him to do what he wanted but after one particularly disastrous outing against a very strong team, he decided that goaltending might not be his thing. He became a forward and it wasn't long before he developed a preference for the other end of the ice. Jari Kurri was his new favourite and scoring was the new focus. Mike went on to play at the elite level for many years. More than twenty years later he is still involved and has embarked on a new career as a coach.

Mike's interest in the game was picked up by his two younger brothers and we have been a committed hockey family for many years. It wasn't long before my many trips driving to the rink led to a rekindled interest in participating and when a coaching position became available, I jumped at the chance. I have been at it ever since. I started by getting involved with my son's novice teams and as they grew older, I began coaching at higher and higher levels. Presently I am coaching a junior team.

Along the way, I became a student of the game and I have read many hockey books. I've also been to a lot of coaching conferences. I usually walk away from these conferences energized and excited about the great new ideas that I have been able to acquire. One thing that has always struck me about the fraternity of hockey coaches is their willingness to share. The overall philosophy, in my observation, has been that if there is more knowledge and quality coaching out there, the game is much better off.

It is in that spirit that I have undertaken this project. For sure there are many coaches out there who have coached at a higher level than I have and there are those who have been around the game for much longer than me, but I have been an educator for many years and I'm hoping that with that background, I will be able to effectively organize and present ideas that will be of benefit to coaches at all levels. One thing that I noticed during my years as a coach is that although there is some very good material available for coaches, there doesn't seem to be anything that takes you chronologically through a "year in the life of a hockey coach."

The title my project is "The Season" and my idea is to work through the stages of the hockey season and share ideas and opinions as I go along. I set out to create the type of resource book that would have been of great benefit to me as I was "learning the ropes" and hopefully, as the subtitle suggests, it will be a blueprint that will be helpful for coaches as they go through their planning. Ideally it will be read from beginning to end and then used periodically as a reference. I have, however, tried to write the book in a manner that lends itself to the reader jumping in at any point and pulling out the information that is needed. If you have already chosen your team, for example, you could leave the "Preparation" and "Evaluation" chapters for later and jump right in to the "Practices" and "Games" chapters.

I am anticipating that it is coaches who will be most interested in the following pages although I believe that it will also appeal to those who have a sincere interest in the game of hockey and just want to learn more ... a parent, perhaps, who is experiencing the game for the first time with an eager young player. Whatever your objective is, I sincerely hope that you find the material useful. Thank you for reading my book and if you have any thoughts and opinions about it ... or ideas that I could integrate into future editions ...please contact me. I would be very interested in hearing from you. (e-mail: ringrosed@macewan.ca). I must say that writing this has been a great way to organize my thoughts and an extremely valuable learning experience in itself. I look forward to future opportunities to acquire even more knowledge and insight about this great game.

Dedication:

To my Dad who introduced me to the game that of hockey and inspired me by playing well into his seventies. To my Mom who has always encouraged me as a player, coach and now as a writer. To my wife Lorraine who endured and supported the years of hectic hockey schedules involving a coach and three elite players. To my sons Michael, Mark and Sean who, as players, have provided me with many years of enjoyment and pride.

Acknowledgements:

First of all, I'd like to acknowledge the many great people who I have encountered during my years of involvement in hockey.

- *Hockey Alberta and the other organizations that have given me the opportunity to coach.*
- *The hard working volunteers whose organizational efforts are largely unrewarded but are so very essential.*
- *The fine parents who have supported my programs and encouraged their children.*
- *The great coaches who I have had the pleasure of working with and learning from.*
- *The efficient team managers who have made my life as a coach so much easier.*
- *The many young players, who have worked hard, had fun and made my trips to the rink so enjoyable.*

In particular, I would like to thank my friend Mark Blair who has been with me nearly every step of the way.

From an organizational point of view, I'd like to acknowledge the University of Alberta Golden Bears hockey team. Clare Drake, Billy Moores, Rob Daum and Eric Thurston along with the many other great coaches and players who have been involved with the team have established and maintained a tradition that is second to none. It has been my pleasure to observe and learn from the organization and they were always very generous with their time when, as a coach, I had questions.

In terms of writing this book, I will first mention my son Mike, who I regularly have great hockey discussions with. Rick Carriere, a friend and mentor in recent years, has also been a great resource. Both were very helpful as I developed this material. Norm Cowley, who was my team manager for many years and more recently has done some fine statistical analysis for me, has also provided me with some valuable opinions and insights. My sister Leslie Sproule, a professional synchronized swimming coach, offered some great ideas and feedback from the perspective of another sport. Last but not least my Mom, Sheila Ringrose, provided an eagle eye in the editing department.

Thank you all so very much for your contributions!!

Table of Contents:

Chapter 1
Preparation

"If you don't know where you are going,
you might end up someplace else"

- Yogi Berra, Baseball Manager

"Chance favours the prepared mind"

- Louis Pasteur, Scientist

"The will to prepare to win is infinitely more important than
the will to win. A team that is really willing to prepare is the
team that has the best chance to win … and wants to win"

- Bobby Knight, Basketball Coach

"By failing to prepare, you are preparing to fail."

- Abraham Lincoln, US President

To get your season off to a successful start, everyone involved with the team needs to arrive prepared. Years ago, training camp was looked at as the time that coaches, support staff and players started getting ready for the season. Today it begins long before that.

This chapter will be written in two parts. In the first segment, we will talk about the preparation needed by the coaches and support staff. In the second segment, we will look at the preparation required by the players.

Coach Preparation

"My job as a coach is to identify each player's strengths and special gifts, and devise a game plan to make each player successful and to ultimately make the team successful."

- George Kingston, Hockey Coach*

* Throughout my book and denoted with an asterisk, I have added quotes from Simply the Best – Insights and Strategies from Great Hockey Coaches. www.SimplyTheBest.com. This book is a compilation by Ryan Walter and Mike Johnston of their interviews with some hockey coaching legends.

The head coach is the ultimate coordinator of the team's plan. Therefore, it is essential that he or she is comfortable with, and is able to work effectively with, the other coaches and support staff. Chemistry is the key word and it is as important off the ice as it is on the ice.

In the coaching staff, it is important to have a good blend of knowledge and people skills. You need to be able to analyze your team and your opponent and develop the appropriate technical preparation and strategy, but it doesn't go anywhere if you are unable to communicate it to your players and get them to commit to it!

Specific roles vary depending on the team and the personnel who are involved with it, but to be effective you should consider the following ingredients:

- *Technical understanding* – Good analysis can lead to improvement and ultimately better performance. There are two parts to this. First of all, you need people who can analyze individual skills. Players will continually improve if you can break down the mechanics of what they do and give them suggestions for practice and improvement. Secondly, you need people who can analyze the composition of the team and determine what tactics and strategies are appropriate. This is obviously very important for the development of your own team but as you get into game situations, it is also very important in the analysis of the opposition. The individuals who have this skill are usually referred to as the ones who are "good with x's and o's." It could be the head coach or one of the assistants. Maybe he or she is the one who breaks down game films or watches the game from the stands.

- *Energy* – If you ask a coach what is feared most or what is cherished most during the course of a game, you will very likely get the same response … momentum. You love to have it and you hate to see the other team get it. It has been the determining factor in countless hockey games. There are individuals who are particularly gifted in creating the energy on a hockey team that leads to momentum and they will be valuable members of your coaching staff.

- *Creativity* – As with any game, a team is sometimes on the attack and at other times it is defending. Sometimes things are going well and at other times there are big problems. Coaches who are able to develop creative ideas and strategies in these situations are likely to be very successful. The ability to come up with something new …"to think outside the box" … is an extremely valuable skill.

- *Communication skills* - This important ingredient can be broken down into two areas. It is, of course, very important to be able to communicate the strategy to your team. The ability to articulate instructions to the team in a concise and clear manner is very important given the limited time that a coach often has. In addition to that, you will often need to have one-on-one discussions with individual players. Some people have a special knack for getting others to open up to discuss problems and concerns. This skill is very helpful for smoothing out the stormy waters that arise at times during the long hockey season.

- *Discipline* – There are a lot of players on a hockey team and getting them all to focus in the right direction is often difficult. Some coaches are particularly good at setting boundaries and keeping a tight lid on anything that may lead players astray. Be careful not to take this concept to extremes, however, as it can wear players down. On the other hand, coaches who don't set adequate disciplinary standards are asking for future performance and attitude problems. Coming up with the right balance is very important.

- *Sense of humour* – The hockey season is a long grind and although your players and staff are involved because they enjoy it, there are times when the pressure and stress can be extremely intense. Individuals who can lighten the mood with a joke or a story are very important at these critical times.

I have seen successful teams spread out these ingredients in many different ways. In addition to the head coach and assistants, trainers, equipment managers, management and other support personnel can all play a part. Many take on more than one role. The bottom line from a planning point of view is to be sure that all the ingredients are there!

Once the proper personnel are in place, it is important to prepare a plan for the season. There are some components of the plan that are definite and you can be quite specific. There are other components that are indefinite and you can't do much more than jot down a few rough ideas. A plan can change as time goes by, however, and so what you develop prior to the season can be looked at as a starting point that will evolve as the season wears on.

Your plan should consist of whatever will benefit you and the team. Exactly what is included for one coach will quite likely differ from what another will use but there will be many similarities.

"Coaching kids in (minor hockey or in) junior is no different from the best teams in the National Hockey League. It is about fundamentals: Have fun coming to the rink, outwork the opposition, help the players be as good as they can be."

- Brian Sutter, Hockey Coach*

Here are some items that are frequently included as part of a seasonal plan:

- Timeline for the season that identifies times for tryouts, exhibition games, regular season games, playoffs and major competitions.
- Identification of personnel and other requirements for evaluation of players during tryouts. Cut down deadlines (both self imposed and league imposed) should be clear. Desirable times for exhibition games should be identified and then a specific schedule should be prepared.
- A schedule of practices, games and off-ice activities (i.e. dryland training, player meetings). Look for gaps in the schedule that may need to be filled. On the other hand, watch for times that appear to be too hectic. Activities may need to be reduced if it appears that players may get burned out.
- Skill development requirements of players. Decide when, during the season, specific skills will be introduced and worked on.
- System development requirements of the team. Consider when and how the team systems (for example the forecheck, power play, etc.) will be introduced and practiced.
- Assignment of routines and responsibilities on practice days, game days and for team activities. Be careful here. One of the pitfalls of inexperienced coaches is that they to try to do too many things on their own. It is interesting to note that in most of the interviews from the book "Simply the Best," the coaches state that when they first began coaching, they tried to do many things themselves. They all go on to say, however, that as they have evolved as coaches they delegate much more and empower those who are on their staff ... and they view themselves as better coaches because of it.
- A schedule with dates and times for regular staff meetings. As stated previously, the seasonal plan will likely change over time and it is important

to get regular input about changes from all members of your staff.
- A schedule of dates and times for regular captain's meetings so that it is possible to get regular player input.

Player Preparation

Moving on to the players, pre-season preparation can be placed in three categories:
1. Acquiring the necessary skills
2. Physical training
3. Mental training

In the next segment of the chapter, we will talk about some of the things that a player can do to enhance readiness in each category.

Acquiring the necessary skills

In his autobiography, Wayne Gretzky talks about the great backyard rink that his Dad built for him every winter. He also talks about playing indoor hockey with his grandmother ... using her legs as goal posts. Looking at this environment, you can see that two very important factors were in place and they obviously contributed to his development as a hockey player ... fun and opportunity. He developed his love of the game because his grandmother took the time to play with him and make it fun. His Dad made a huge contribution to his enjoyment with all of the work that went into the backyard rink. It also gave Wayne an opportunity to play as much hockey as possible and thus he was able to spend a lot of time honing his skills.

I believe that skill acquisition begins as soon as a player has his or her first exposure to hockey ... maybe even before he or she straps on his or her first pair of skates. By the time my youngest son Sean was old enough to sit up and take notice of what was going on around him, his older brothers were playing organized hockey. Every Saturday, Sean was part of the excitement of getting his brothers dressed for the game, driving to the arena, cheering for the players on the ice and probably having a little post game treat on the way home. It was an enjoyable experience for him and it wasn't long before he became really intrigued with what was happening on the ice. I can remember him sitting on my wife's knee intently watching the players as they skated back and forth.

Fast forward a couple of years and Sean is approaching his third birthday. He asks for a pair of skates for Christmas. Santa Claus obliged and the very next day I took him out for his first skate. I had a small chair all ready for him to push along the ice ... for support as he took his first steps. It was a technique that had worked well for his two brothers. I was prepared for the sore back that would surely follow as I bent over to steady him in his early skating efforts.

A remarkable thing happened, however. I laced up his brother's skates and they took off onto the ice. Then, I laced up Sean's skates and as I turned to get the chair, he stood up and went on to the ice himself. Before I could get there to help him, he had taken his first steps and away he went! Without any problem at all, he was off and skating!

I relate this story because I think that it illustrates some interesting things about skill development. First of all, observation is a powerful tool and we can learn a lot about a skill by just watching it. Secondly, Sean was extremely motivated to get out there and skate and it was because he perceived skating as being fun. The stage was now set and I did everything that I could to give him opportunities to do more of it. He never looked back and to this day he loves to go to the rink.

I would insert caution at this point because parents sometimes get over zealous in their attempts to expose their children to more and more hockey. It is pretty easy to overload a young player and if that happens, going to the rink is likely to become a chore rather than an enjoyable experience. It is probable that decreased motivation will cause skill development to suffer ... if the player wants to continue playing at all!

I remember taking the boys to a public skate at one of the local arenas one Saturday afternoon and as we were playing a game of tag on the ice, I noticed some parents sitting in the stands with a few of their friends. They were watching a young boy (probably about 5 years of age) as he skated around the ice with a little hockey stick and a puck. He had remarkable skills. Periodically, his Dad would shout ... "Do a Gretzky!" or "Do a Lemieux!" and the boy would execute a fancy maneuver to the delight of his spectators. Later on, as we were getting our skates off, I overheard his Mother telling the friends about all of the skating lessons that the young fellow was going to. I watched the little guy on and off the ice and didn't detect a lot of joy as he went through his routines all by himself. He was willing to be at the rink but didn't seem to be having a lot of fun there.

A few years later this young man was heavily involved in minor hockey. He was tearing up the league in scoring and there was even a newspaper article written about the young phenomenon. The sky seemed to be the limit and his parents were just ecstatic as they told everyone who would listen about his great accomplishments. Over time an interesting thing happened, though. As he grew older, he became much less dominant and the last time I remember watching him play a game was at the peewee level. He was only about twelve years of age but sadly he looked like the most disinterested player on the ice. He still had great skills but it was obvious that his desire wasn't there. It wasn't much longer before he quit the game.

So if the objective is to maximize skill development while ensuring that the player is having fun and cultivating a love of the game, how is that accomplished? Well here are a few of my thoughts:

Provide the opportunity. We've talked about that already. Remember, though, that opportunity doesn't mean more classes. It doesn't hurt to be involved in some of these but in my opinion the best thing that you can do is take your young player and a bunch of friends to the rink for some good old fashioned shinny. Better still, participate yourself!

Take power skating classes. Learning proper technique pays huge dividends as players develop. Skating is the most important skill in hockey and rightfully it should be given more attention than others. Again I will insert a word of caution, however. Some power skating instructors are very good at making this experience a lot of fun while others just go through the motions and their students quickly lose interest. Make sure to do your research before enrolling your child!

Take some skill development classes. There seem to be more and more specialty classes emerging these days ... for example puck handling, shooting and checking. Again, these can be helpful in developing proper technique. In recent years, many hockey academies have sprung up. These allow players to develop hockey skills as part of their daily school curriculum. I have seen some remarkable development in players who have attended these schools but again I would insert a word of caution in terms of overload. That much focus on one sport isn't for everyone!

Play summer hockey? I make this point with a question mark because there are different opinions about whether it is a positive or a negative. The advantage of summer hockey is that it gives elite players an opportunity to play with the best and learn from them. Almost everyone seems to be doing it these days and so it can give the player a great opportunity for further development. Supporters of summer hockey will usually justify it by concluding that if the youngster loves the game so much, then why not? Certainly I have seen a lot of players show great improvement through their participation in summer hockey. One disadvantage, of course, is that you are risking burnout. Players arrive at tryout camp with virtually no break from hockey since the prior season and it is very difficult for them to maintain their intensity.

The one great example that comes to mind when I hear questions about whether you really need summer hockey is Mike Fogolin, son of former NHL defenceman Lee Fogolin. Mike loved to play the game of hockey. When you watched him on the ice, you could just tell how much he enjoyed playing. I'm sure that he would have loved to have played summer hockey but his parents Lee and Carol discouraged it believing that it was important to be involved in other activities. Mike arrived at tryouts every year just full of enthusiasm after a good long rest. He always stepped in … never missing a beat … and if you were to look at development over the season, there was nobody who progressed more than Mike. Rather than tailing off like some of the players who had never had a break, he just kept getting better. He sailed through his minor hockey years and became a great young defenceman for the Prince George Cougars of the Western Hockey League. I have no doubt that he would have been an excellent NHL defenceman had he not died suddenly and tragically due to a heart problem.

I contrast this to another story about a young man who was the same age as my youngest son Sean. This fellow … I will call him Tom … played in a summer league that ran two to three times a week throughout the summer months. It wasn't that Tom didn't enjoy himself. It was a league that was a bit less serious than some summer hockey programs and Tom was a dominant player. He won the scoring title nearly every year and when the league wrapped up, he went straight into tryouts for winter teams. Because he had been playing all summer he was, of course, at the top of his game. The trouble was that when you saw him at tryouts it was usually as good as he was going to get for the season. Once everyone else caught up in terms of conditioning and intensity, Tom looked very ordinary. At the end of the season he was often near the top of the scoring race but when you had a really good look at it, most of the points were accumulated in the first few months. He was usually invisible by playoff time.

Nonetheless, the scouts always got a good first impression of Tom and when it was his year in the Bantam draft, he was selected in the first round. To prepare Tom, for the Western Hockey league, he played the next season in the major midget league with players who were mostly two years older than he was and then he made the jump to major junior as a sixteen year old. It just never seemed to work out for him there and after three frustrating seasons of trying to live up to his potential Tom lost his self confidence and eventually quit hockey. The bottom line was that this was a player who was probably slightly above average. He may have really excelled with the right sort of developmental approach but in the attempt to put him on the fast track to success, he got in over his head and eventually burned out.

Additional pitfalls when considering participation in summer hockey are the cost and the time commitment required. In terms of cost, hockey is very expensive as it is. Making it a year round activity just intensifies the problem. In terms of time, it will probably be necessary for players to sacrifice other activities. We will discuss this more in the next section.

Whatever you decide, summer hockey is popular and is here to stay. So far, Canadian Hockey (the governing body) has refused to support the activity believing that it is too much for young players. Recently, however, they have softened their stance and they are now supporting some creative activities (for example "three-on-three" hockey leagues and tournaments) that will provide a change of pace and yet still give players some ice time during the off season.

Get involved in other sporting activities (cross training). As people get very heavily involved in one sport, they generally have no time for participation in others. That is such a shame! Not only are they sacrificing the mental break that these activities provide but there are so many acquired skills that transfer very well to the game of hockey. Furthermore, a player who has experience in other sports is often more creative. Jari Kurri, the Oiler forward who had so many great years playing alongside Wayne Gretzky, credits soccer as a huge factor in his development as a player. Puck handling, passing and playmaking were all hockey skills that were enhanced by his related soccer skills. Another example who comes to mind is former Calgary Flame Joe Niewendyk. He was an elite lacrosse player. The skills that he developed playing that sport (quick hands, good hand-eye coordination) helped him become one of the game's best puck handlers.

Here is a list of just a few sports that a young player might be interested in pursuing along with some thoughts re: the cross-training benefits that might be realized in his or her development as a hockey player.

- Basketball – agility, quickness
- Golf – understanding of body mechanics (i.e. weight transfer for shooting the puck), mental toughness
- Cycling, jogging, rollerblading – leg strength for quick acceleration, endurance
- Skateboarding – balance, toughness (you've got to be tough to handle some of those wipeouts!)
- Swimming – strength (particularly upper body strength), cardiovascular training
- Football, rugby – toughness, body contact technique
- Boxing, wrestling – strength, quickness
- Ball hockey, roller hockey – puck handling, vision of the ice, positional play

As a coach, I also find that when my players are familiar with other sports, it helps them to have a better understanding of the game of hockey. It is sometimes easier to explain one concept when you can relate it to another. Man to man basketball coverage is similar to the man to man defensive zone coverage that some hockey teams use. The picks and screens that are often used as offensive hockey tactics are also similar to basketball strategies. I like to refer to my defencemen as being similar to football quarterbacks who are looking for the open man to pass to as they initiate a breakout from the defensive zone. There are many other examples.

Finally, players who participate in other sports are often better all around athletes and their level of conditioning is often superior to those who don't. Again I can relate a personal story to support that. My middle son Mark likes to play hockey but has a lot of other sporting interests. He is a big fan of skateboarding and inline skating and in the summer prior to his final year of Bantam hockey he spent most of his time out on the pavement working on his technique in those activities. Most of his hockey peers were busy with hockey camps and summer teams but Mark just needed to have a rest and so he decided to stay away from the rink. When it came to tryouts, I was expecting him to be a bit rusty but on the contrary, he showed great acceleration and a powerful stride that had not been as noticeable in previous years. In addition to that, he was hitting harder because of the great leg strength that he had developed. He went on to have his best season ever!

Physical Training

With respect to physical readiness, I have noted a huge increase in off-season workout activity in recent years. It has been an important part of a professional hockey player's life for a while now, and it is not surprising that college and junior teams have jumped on the bandwagon by designing off-season training programs for their players, but it has filtered down even further than that. Minor hockey players have started off-season training at a very early age.

As a coach, you can put your players onto the right track by integrating some dry-land training into your seasonal plan. For the older players, there are many fitness consultants out there who are able to design excellent hockey-specific training that is aimed at improving the strength, agility and cardiovascular levels of athletes. For the younger players, experts will tell you to be careful what you do. Strength training using weights, for example, can lead to problems if attempted by players whose muscles and bones are still developing unless proper technique is used. However, there are many strength building exercises that do not involve the use of weights.

When I was coaching Atom hockey, we used to set aside some time each week after our on-ice practices to give the players a bit of exposure to training. One week we'd do a bit of cardiovascular training (running the stands of the arena, skipping, etc.). The next week we'd work on our strength (pushups, sit-ups, etc.). Sometimes we'd do some agility training with light plyometrics (again it is necessary to be mindful that too much of that activity is not advisable for those who have developing muscles and bones). Other times we'd work on something hockey specific (i.e. stick handling routines with golf balls). There are lots of creative ideas out there. We'd set up competitions, have some music blaring and the guys would have a good time just hanging out together. The young athletes were tested at the beginning and at the end of the season and they were able to monitor their progress.

Did these training sessions help our fitness level? Well, at that age I am sure that they helped a bit ... but not really dramatically. They definitely provided some other benefits, however, and they apply directly to the concept of physical readiness. First of all, they helped show the players that training didn't have to be a chore. The players really looked forward to the sessions and they developed some good training habits that were carried with them into the off-season. Secondly, it was a great team builder. Of course they got to know one another better but we also observed that as players competed and compared results in the pursuit of their goals, friendly rivalries developed and they pushed one another to higher levels of accomplishment. I still get some satisfaction when I see my former players who are now playing junior, college and even professional hockey going to the gym in groups during the off-season ... likely enjoying the camaraderie and pushing each other just like they used to after practices many years ago!

Mental Training
Mental training is another area that has shown a recent increase in popularity. Here are some techniques that you frequently hear about as being effectively integrated into an athlete's preparation.

Goal Setting. This is a powerful tool. It is certainly effective for athletes but it is a skill that translates well to other activities so it is also a great life skill. As a college instructor, I have found that athletes are often very good students and I believe that their ability to set goals is a primary reason why. By establishing a benchmark to strive for, it focuses attention and increases motivation. This leads to a very positive effect on performance.

As a coach, I have used goal setting extensively with players of all ages. My first step is to divide the season into segments and have the players set team goals for each segment. The first segment is entitled "**establishing discipline and gaining respect**" and the objective is to establish team norms, routines, and systems that will help us become successful as a team. The second segment is entitled "**commitment to excellence**" and the focus is to fine tune our individual and team performances in preparation for the home stretch of the season. The third segment is entitled "**championship focus**" and as the name suggests, we do everything we can to ensure success in our end-of-season playoffs and tournaments. Each segment takes up roughly one third of the season.

As we approach each segment, we set specific team goals. I have used the following categories ... win/loss record, placement in the standings, goals for and against per game, shots for and against per game, hits per game, plus/minus performance, power play percentage, penalty kill percentage, face-off percentage, penalty minutes per game, save percentage and goals against average (for the goaltenders). There are certainly others that can be used. I make sure that everyone participates in the goal setting process and we come to as much of a group consensus as we can.

Once the players have worked together on team goals, I have them identify what they can do as individuals to contribute to the success of the team. In other words, they set individual goals for the segment. Once the goals are set, we monitor them very closely. After games, I encourage the players to take some time at home to think about the game and fill out a one page worksheet. They give themselves and the team a grade and then answer some simple questions ... What did I do well? What can I improve on? What did the team do well? What can the team improve on?

When setting goals, there are some guidelines to keep in mind. First of all, the goals need to be **specific**. Setting numbers as a target (i.e. 8 wins out of the next 12 games) rather than a general goal like "we need to play better" ensures that players know exactly what is to be achieved. Secondly, the goals need to be **measurable**. If you are going to set a goal like shots on goal then ensure that there is somebody keeping track of the shots! Thirdly, goals need to be **attainable**. You want to challenge your players but if you set standards ridiculously high it won't take long for players to get frustrated and the goal will lose its motivational effect. Fourthly, the goals should be *results-oriented*. In other words, they should support what the team is trying to accomplish. A player goal to get into a fight every game, for example, might be good for his ego but is it something that will help the team win? … probably not. Finally, goals should be *time-bound*. Whether it is an individual game or a segment of games, the period of time for completion of the goals should be clearly specified. Putting it all together, we can simply say that goals need to be SMART … *specific, measurable, attainable, results-oriented and time-bound.*

The following exhibits provide examples of a completed goal setting worksheet and a completed game evaluation worksheet that I used when I was coaching Bantam hockey.

Goal Setting Worksheet

 **WEST EDMONTON WILD**

Second Segment Goals

Name: Wayne Burns
Position: Right Wing

Personal Goals

List your goals for the second segment of the season (12 games):

	Per Game	In Total
Shots on goal	4	48
Goals		14
Assists		16
Plus / Minus	1	12
Hits / Takeouts	4	48
Giveaways		6
Faceoff Percentage		N/A
Save Percentage		N/A
Goals Against		N/A
Other		No bad penalties

Team Goals

List the goals that you would like to see the team reach for the second segment:

Shots per game	More than 30
Goals per game	3 or more
Shots against per game	Less than 30
Goals against per game	2 or less
Powerplay Percentage	20% or higher
Penalty Kill Percentage	85% or higher
Penalty Minutes	16 minutes or fewer
Faceoff Percentage	60% or higher
Win – Loss Record	8 wins – 4 losses or better
Plus / Minus	80% of the team even or better

WEST EDMONTON WILD

Game Evaluation Sheet

Date of Game: January 14
Opponent: Maple Leafs
Score: 5 – 2 Win

Name: Wayne Burns

1. **Individual Grade:** __B+__ (A, B, C or D)

2. **What did I do well?**
   Played well defensively. Worked hard, made some hits, blocked some shots. Had no goals against when I was on the ice.

3. **What can I improve on?**
   Offensive production. I didn't achieve my shots on goal target. I need to win more battles for the puck in the offensive corners and in front of the net. Only one assist for the game.

4. **Team Grade:** __A-__ (A, B, C or D)

5. **What did the team do well?**
   Took advantage of scoring opportunities. Played pretty well defensively. Good penalty killing. Great goaltending.

6. **What can the team improve on?**
   Took too many penalties. Gave up too many shots against. Faceoff percentage was too low.

I have found that players will respond to goal setting at any level. They enjoy the process. Having them fill out forms regularly keeps them focused and then having regular team meetings to discuss our progress keeps motivation very high. Game by game, I also find that it is easier to develop strategy and create action plans when goals are clearly in place.

Because it is a long season, I do things to provide some variety. For example, I may change the forms slightly from segment to segment, I may have meetings prior to games rather than after practices, I may have players hand in the forms rather than discuss them at a team meeting. The objective of this is to keep it fresh and interesting and thus realize maximum benefit from the process.

A final thought on goals is that you should be careful not to look at winning, especially at the beginning of the season, as the only true measure of success. I like winning as much as the next guy but in order to be successful, many of the goals need to focus on player development. Ultimately only one team can win the championship but you can be successful every year if you can observe individual players and the team improving over the season.

"Success is best measured as a journey in performance improvement. My bottom line definition of success is very simply "playing with the passion to be the best you can be."

-- George Kingston, Hockey Coach*

Visualization. This can also be a very powerful tool. Formulating a mental picture of what you want to accomplish prior to the actual performance is the objective. It can be done at practice, prior to the game or even on the bench during the game and like any skill, the more the athlete works at it, the more effective it becomes.

As a coach, there are things that you can do to introduce the athlete to visualization. Talking about the process provides an introduction but to be really effective, it is something that needs to be experienced. I periodically take my players through a visualization exercise prior to games. I have them sit quietly with their eyes closed or else I have them put their gloves on the floor and lie back with their head on the gloves and feet on the dressing room bench. I then take them through some deep breathing to relax and open up their subconscious mind. While they are in this state, they are very susceptible to vivid visualization and I encourage them to imagine themselves having a great warm up and then performing well during the game. Making a nice pass, taking a shot, blocking a shot, making a great check or, for a goaltender, making a spectacular save are all examples of visualizations that can be encouraged. I usually finish the session off by suggesting that they visualize the scoreboard at the end of the game. An example of the wording that I may use to guide the visualization is found at the end of the chapter.

I have a great memory of the first time that I used this technique with a team. I was coaching an Atom team and we were participating in Minor Hockey Week which is a huge mid season tournament in Edmonton that attracts a lot of press coverage and much excitement in the city's minor hockey community. We had a young team made up primarily of first year players in our age group and although we were very talented, we had a difficult time competing against most other teams in our division who were comprised primarily of second year players. One team in particular was very strong. The coach had recruited players from all over the city. It was mid January and they had not lost a game all year. As luck would have it, this was the team that we drew for our first tournament game.

I had a great group of kids and they were very responsive to new ideas, so I thought that I would try a little visualization prior to the game. We went through the process and once we were finished, I detected a little extra spark as we skated onto the ice. After a good warm up we started into the game and I was amazed at the level that the kids were playing at. We put in our best performance of the season and to make a long story short we knocked the big boys off of their pedestal with a dramatic goal in the last few minutes of the game. It was a Cinderella story for our young team and I'm convinced that the visualization exercise played a large part in helping to put them in the right mindset. They believed that they could beat this undefeated team and when they took the ice, they all had a clear picture of how they were going to do it!

Emotional Control. Hockey is an extremely emotional game. The adrenaline that pumps through the body as the speed and intensity of the game rises can take performance levels to great heights. If not channeled effectively, however, it can lead to lack of discipline on the part of individual players and eventually to the whole team. Once a team gets into penalty trouble they begin focusing on the refereeing and the dirty tactics of the other team. This takes focus away from systems and individual responsibilities and it isn't long before performance suffers. Frequently, the other team starts to build momentum. This, in turn, leads to frustration and continued lack of discipline and it becomes a vicious circle.

One of the essential responsibilities of the coach is to monitor the emotions of his or her team and attempt to make adjustments as necessary. Players need to understand when they need to use their emotions to lift up their intensity and conversely when they have to rein in their emotions to avoid undisciplined penalties or unproductive behaviour. Sometimes, there are things that need to be said to the team. Sometimes, there are certain individuals who require one-on-one attention. It is the effective coach who will know when to step in and what approach to take. It is also important to remember that as a role model, the team will often follow your lead. Sometimes that will work to your advantage but if you lose control, it can just as easily be detrimental!

If you follow effective teams over the course of a season or during a playoff run you will note that they never get too high after a win and they never get too low after a loss. This is part of having good emotional control. If you get too high it can lead to overconfidence and the likelihood that you will let your guard down and take future opponents too lightly. If you get too low there can easily be a loss of confidence and the resulting anxiety leads to costly mistakes that have a negative effect on performance.

Affirmation. A quality that you will always see in a champion is the "can do" attitude ... sometimes called efficacy. It is the firm belief that you can be successful. For some it almost comes naturally without effort but for most it is a skill that is learned and cultivated over time. Minor hockey coaches have the best opportunity to foster the development of the right attitude. The older people get, the more they rely on old habits and it is harder to make changes. Young players are just like sponges and they will absorb whatever they witness and get an opportunity to practice on a regular basis.

Promoting affirmation is often a very subtle process. Off-hand comments like "I can't do that" or "we suck" need to be addressed and corrected immediately. If they are allowed to stand, it doesn't take long for a negative attitude to sink in and it can spread around a team like wildfire. Team members can either create energy or drain energy. Coaches need to emphasize the former and minimize the latter.

It is useful for young players to observe television interviews with elite amateur or professional athletes. Even though these players may privately have doubts, outwardly there is never a hint of belief that there will be anything but success in the future. Even when the situation looks grim, they shift the focus on what needs to be done to turn the tide and realize success.

The great coaches who were interviewed in "Simply the Best" had many things to say about the importance of being positive and in particular, they emphasized proper body language and positive self-talk as being important to watch for in their players. As coaches, we can continually teach and emphasize these techniques in the dressing room, on the bench and between games and in doing so, we will very likely see an improvement in performance.

"You talk to yourself thousands of times in a day. We tried to get the players to make as much of it as possible by being positive and focusing on the good things they do."

- Clare Drake, Hockey Coach*

As a sports fan, I find it fascinating observing athletes in pressure situations. Some are able to take their game to a higher level while others make mistakes that ultimately are the difference between winning and losing. You can observe it in any sport but I find that it is most dramatically observable in the game of golf ... and particularly on the last few holes of a major championship.

Golf is unique because the amount of time that you actually spend performing is very small compared to the time that you have to think about it. There may only be a ten foot putt that a player has to make to win the tournament but what about the time that he or she has to think about it? While preparing for that final shot the player must continue to focus positively on the goal (sinking the putt, winning the tournament). Likely there is a visualization of the putt going into the hole and sometimes you can see the self-talk that affirms their ability to do it. Emotional control is necessary so the nerves don't have a negative impact on the physical skills that are required to execute the putt and the player has to firmly believe that he or she will be successful. If that control isn't there, you can often see it by reading their body language. There are many ways for the player's thinking to get sidetracked and you see many examples of shots missed because the mental toughness wasn't there but just as many times you will marvel at the ability of these athletes to hold it together and perform successfully despite the great pressure that they are facing.

I believe that mental training plays a huge role in separating the achievers from the non-achievers, the champions from the also-rans. Tiger Woods is a phenomenal athlete. His conditioning and technical skills are as good as anyone in the game, but his mental toughness is what takes him to the next level of superstardom. If you look at the pro golf tour before Tiger arrived on the scene, Greg Norman had the skills and the physical prowess to be as dominant then as Tiger is now. He did have a very good professional career but he never quite reached the level that was expected of him. Time and time again he was very close in a major tournament but in so many instances, he found a way to let it slip from his grasp. Watching him on television, you could see that the mental toughness in these situations was lacking. Sports psychologists are the professionals who support athletes in the development of mental toughness and as their great value is recognized, they are increasingly utilized by individuals and teams.

The following paragraphs give you an example of the type wording that I use to lead a pre-game visualization. It starts with some quick words to relax the body and open up the subconscious mind and then inserts some suggestions to heighten anticipation, create positive images and tone the brain and the body. The end of the session reawakens the player and sets the stage for a great performance. This is just an outline … it can, of course be modified as necessary. I usually find that a three to five minute session works quite well.

"Close your eyes, relax your body and breathe deeply. As you take each deep breath, feel the air inflating your lungs to their full capacity. With each deep breath the oxygen enters your blood stream and is carried to every part of your body. Feel its energizing effect. With each deep breath your muscles, bones, tendons and ligaments are getting more prepared. With each deep breath your mind is clearer, your senses are sharper. Your body is ready for peak performance. Quietly take a few more deep breaths and feel yourself getting more and more energized for the upcoming game.

As you continue to breathe deeply, visualize yourself out on the ice for the pre-game warm-up. Your body has never felt better. There is a jump in your skating stride. You glide effortlessly around the ice, feeling the power of every stride. Now feel the stick in your hand. It feels lighter than usual. Your hands feel soft as you give and receive passes. The puck is on your stick like glue as you carry it and off your stick like a rocket as you pass and shoot. Continue to breathe deeply and visualize the buzz of excitement of the warm-up. The cool fresh air energizes you even further. Admire the speed and accuracy of your shot as you are shooting … or marvel at how clearly you are seeing the puck and how easily you are making saves if you are the goaltender. Look around the building, feel the excitement and anticipation in the air. You can hardly wait for the game to start.

Now feel your body getting stronger and feel your focus getting even clearer as the game begins. Think about great plays that you have made in the past. See yourself making them regularly during the game. It might be a great save, a nice goal, a spectacular defensive play … you are at the top of your game. The team is in sync. Everybody is contributing. Imagine a goal for your team, then another … see a great defensive play that shuts down the opposition, then another … visualize a great save against their top player, then another. When the team is playing like this it is so clear why you love the game of hockey.

Now after a few more deep breaths visualize the scoreboard at the end of the game. Another great win for the team. Feel the satisfaction. You are totally spent because you left everything on the ice but you are so proud of the team's performance and of your contribution. Enjoy the post-game celebration and experience the camaraderie as you share the moment with your teammates.

Now take a few more deep breaths, feel the energy in your body reaching its maximum level and open your eyes. Look around the room and see the readiness in your teammates. Buckle up those helmets … it is time to turn your visualization into reality!"

Chapter 2
Evaluation

> "How you select people is more important than how you manage them once they are on the job. If you start with the right people, you won't have problems later on"

> - Red Auerbach, Basketball Coach

At one coaching conference I attended, the individual started his presentation on evaluation suggesting that as coaches we just had to "take good guys." It sounds pretty simple but it is true. In my opinion, the most difficult job that a coach faces is choosing the right players. On almost every team that I have coached, I have gotten into the season and looked back at certain choices that I made wondering what I was thinking when I made the selection. Some times the problem is that the individual player isn't capable ... other times, the individual players are all capable but the team chemistry isn't quite right.

If you look at the list of failed draft choices for any NHL team you can quickly conclude that player evaluation and selection is tricky at any level. Hopefully, as people gain experience and develop a better understanding of the game they will make fewer mistakes but perfection would be just about impossible to attain. There are too many variables. Nonetheless, I believe that there are some things that you can do to get the most out of your evaluation. Here are some suggestions:

- *Do your homework* – I have coached elite hockey for close to 20 years and in that time, I can count on one hand the number of coaches who called me up for a scouting report on players that I have coached. That boggles my mind. Why wouldn't you use every resource possible to help you choose your team? Every year that I coach I have many conversations and make numerous phone calls to gather as much information as possible about upcoming players. Sometimes you throw out information because it is biased. Sometimes you get conflicting reports and you aren't sure what to believe. Most times, however, you accumulate information that is very helpful.
- *Have a very organized approach to evaluation* – This is very important. One organization that I coached for had a manual that was given to all coaches with a clear outline of the process. Where that isn't in place, the coach should develop a checklist. Here are some questions for consideration:
  - When does evaluation begin, what are the cut down dates, and when does the team have to be finalized?
  - Who will the evaluators be and do you have enough expertise to evaluate the different positions?
  - What specific skills and attributes are you looking for in players?
  - What is the grading scale and what type of evaluation form will be used?
  - How will results be summarized and compiled?
  - How will the final decisions be made and who will be involved?
- *Consider the big picture* – Decision making can sometimes be one dimensional. Evaluators are so hung up on one type of player that they miss other ingredients that are important to a team. The players that immediately stand out are often the small, fast, offensive-minded ones but a team full of those players isn't going to work. You need size and an element of toughness ... and you need players who are willing to play defence. Yet if you are evaluating purely on skill, you may end up with a

team that is missing those components. At the other end of the scale, evaluators tend to look at hockey as a big man's game. You may get too hung up on building a big, tough team full of foot soldiers and miss the vital skill component.

- *Look and look again!* – Most of the mistakes that I have made in my evaluation decisions are because I am too focused on one characteristic of a hockey player and I may miss other important elements. The beautiful skater who looks great wheeling up and down the ice but isn't willing to get involved physically is one common problem to watch for. Choosing this type of player can give you a season of frustration! On the other side of the coin, you have the player who isn't pretty to watch but is always competitive. You may miss him or her if you aren't watching closely enough! The bottom line is that if you like one thing that a player does, remember that it is just one piece of the puzzle. Have your evaluators look closely at others before you make your final decision.

- *Be aware of off-ice problems* – Nothing can kill team chemistry more quickly than a bad attitude. There may be players who seem to give you everything you need on the ice but their behaviour on the bench and in the dressing room might mean that they are more useful to you if they are playing for another team. Of course you always hear the stories about players who change and as a coach you want to believe that your approach is going to turn the player around. I'm not saying that it can't happen but if you are going to take a chance, make sure that you have a strategy in place to deal with any problems that may arise!

- *Consider what is best for the development of each player* – As players develop, they are continually acquiring new skills. Most of these are quite visible as you watch them on the ice. What isn't as noticeable is the development of a player's confidence and here is where you need to be very careful. If players are pushed along too quickly, they sometimes don't develop the confidence and leadership on the ice that is necessary to compete at the higher levels. Although it is sometimes difficult to accept, it may be better to release a player so that he or she will have the opportunity to be a leader on a lower tier team for a season.

- *Sleep on it* – Some of the selection errors that I have made are as the result of hasty decisions. You want to avoid a phenomenon called "groupthink." It arises when the pressure to make a quick decision prevents the group from critically appraising unusual, minority or unpopular views. In hockey evaluation there is often a time constraint and so the pressure to get the job done may prevent the group from having a closer look at certain players or gathering more information about them. If at all possible, step back, reconsider your evaluator's comments and take time to think about things for a while before you make the final call.

The evaluation process generally begins with large numbers of hopeful players. The first decision is how many of those players should be on the ice at any one time. I have experimented a bit with this and ideally, I like to see 30 players (two teams of nine forwards, four defence and two goaltenders). Of course it is difficult to always have exact numbers so some variation is inevitable but if you go too far over that target it is difficult to give everyone an adequate evaluation and if you go too far below that target it is difficult for most players to keep up the desired intensity for the whole ice session. I have also experimented a bit with the time of each ice session and I would say that 1 ¼ hours is ideal ... especially in the early stages of evaluation. That is usually enough time to get a good look at players but not long enough to burn them out. Again there may be some slight variations to this based on factors like the number of players, the caliber of player being evaluated or the intensity of the workout.

After seeing everyone on the ice once, you should be able to cut the numbers down quite drastically. In order to do that, however, you need to have adequate evaluation drills and an adequate number of evaluators. If you are trying to get a complete picture of players when your drills don't provide evaluators with the opportunity to see vital skills, then things may be missed. Let's say, for example, that your evaluation drills focus on skating and shooting. There is little attention paid to passing or checking. What will you get? Well, chances are your team will look good in the warm up but they will struggle when they are required to play as a team or provide defensive support for their teammates.

There are many skills that are involved in the game of hockey and it might be a good idea to get your evaluators into the right mindset by brainstorming a list of those skills. A working list may look something like this:

Skating: Forward skating, backwards skating, forward crossovers (right and left), backwards crossovers (right and left), stopping (right and left), tight turn (right and left), pivots (back to front and front to back).

Passing: Forehand pass, backhand pass, saucer pass, chip pass, spot pass, cycling pass, receiving a pass (forehand and backhand).

Shooting: Slap shot, wrist shot, backhand shot, one-timer shot, tipped shot.

Checking: Body check, pinning (sealing), stick check, poke check, sweep check, back check (tracking).

Mental: Hockey sense, competitiveness, persistence, sportsmanship, puck support.

Goaltender: Skating ability, lateral movements, balance and agility, positioning and angles, rebound control, use of hands/feet/stick, passing ability, anticipation, net coverage, consistency, mental toughness.

The list of skills should be refined each time the coaching staff goes through the evaluation process. Obviously, depending on the developmental level of players, some skills may be looked at more than others. For example, skating skills would be critical when evaluating younger players who are just learning the game. At higher levels, most players can skate well enough. It may be that other elements are more important to watch for in your particular situation. You may be looking for scoring, for example, if your team from the prior season was having trouble putting the puck in the net!

Here are a couple of evaluation practices that I designed for a recent tryout camp. Although goaltenders are involved in all of the tryout sessions, I like to have a session that allows them and the evaluators to focus on the specific set of skills that they require. When putting the plans together, I started with a list of skills and then included drills that I thought would require the use of as many as possible. I found that posting these on the wall at the entrance to the arena gave the players and evaluators a chance to review them prior to the ice session. It also gave everyone a good preview of the specific skills that were going to be emphasized.

One hour evaluation practice

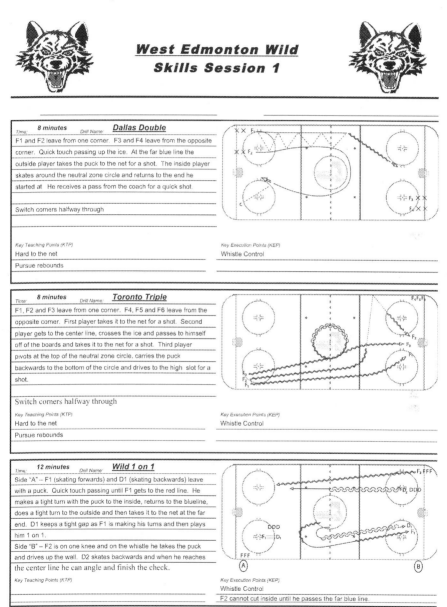

West Edmonton Wild
Skills Session 1

Time: **8 minutes**   *Drill Name:* **Dallas Double**

F1 and F2 leave from one corner. F3 and F4 leave from the opposite corner. Quick touch passing up the ice. At the far blue line the outside player takes the puck to the net for a shot. The inside player skates around the neutral zone circle and returns to the end he started at. He receives a pass from the coach for a quick shot.

Switch corners halfway through

Key Teaching Points (KTP)
Hard to the net
Pursue rebounds

Key Execution Points (KEP)
Whistle Control

Time: **8 minutes**   *Drill Name:* **Toronto Triple**

F1, F2 and F3 leave from one corner. F4, F5 and F6 leave from the opposite corner. First player takes it to the net for a shot. Second player gets to the center line, crosses the ice and passes to himself off of the boards and takes it to the net for a shot. Third player pivots at the top of the neutral zone circle, carries the puck backwards to the bottom of the circle and drives to the high slot for a shot.

Switch corners halfway through

Key Teaching Points (KTP)
Hard to the net
Pursue rebounds

Key Execution Points (KEP)
Whistle Control

Time: **12 minutes**   *Drill Name:* **Wild 1 on 1**

Side "A" -- F1 (skating forwards) and D1 (skating backwards) leave with a puck. Quick touch passing until F1 gets to the red line. He makes a tight turn with the puck to the inside, returns to the blueline, does a tight turn to the outside and then takes it to the net at the far end. D1 keeps a tight gap as F1 is making his turns and then plays him 1 on 1.
Side "B" -- F2 is on one knee and on the whistle he takes the puck and drives up the wall. D2 skates backwards and when he reaches the center line he can angle and finish the check.

Key Teaching Points (KTP)

Key Execution Points (KEP)
Whistle Control
F2 cannot cut inside until he passes the far blue line.

"Dig Deep"

29

Time: **10 minutes**   Drill Name: **_Bear 2 on 1_**

Coach starts the drill with a pass to D1 who shoots from the point. D2 then initiates a 2 on 1 (F1 and F2 against D1). D2 then follows up the play and after the 2 on 1 is complete gets a pass from a coach at the other end of the ice. The drill then proceeds in the opposite direction.

Key Teaching Points (KTP)

Key Execution Points (KEP)
Flow Drill

Time: **8 minutes**   Drill Name: **_Battle Drill_**

1 on 1, 2 on 2 corner battles

Key Teaching Points (KTP)

Key Execution Points (KEP)

Time: **10 minutes**   Drill Name: **_Cross-Ice 3 on 3_**

Key Teaching Points (KTP)

Key Execution Points (KEP)

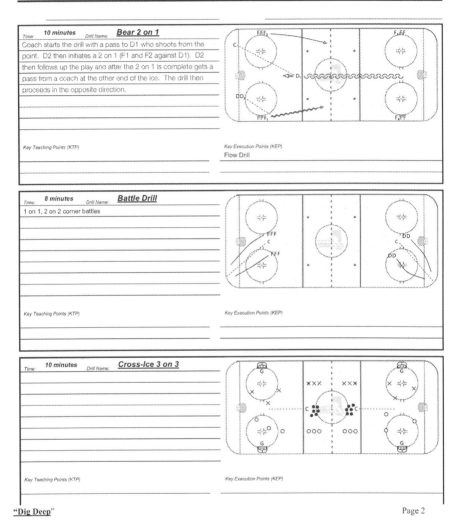

"Dig Deep"

Goaltender evaluation session

West Edmonton Wild
Goaltender Session

Date: _____   **Duration:** _____

Time: **12 minutes**   *Drill Name:* **Goalie Evaluation**

Warmup, stretch, move around the net.

Each goaltender has two minutes in the net to demonstrate
butterfly, post to post, up and downs, telescoping and angles.

Key Teaching Points (KTP)

Key Execution Points (KEP)

Time: **12 minutes**   *Drill Name:* **Goalie Evaluation**

Side "A" -- Rapid fire shooting from the high slot

Side "B" -- Net drives from each side

Key Teaching Points (KTP)

Key Execution Points (KEP)

Time: **12 minutes**   *Drill Name:* **Goalie Evaluation**

Side "A" – Shuttle Drill. Shooter 1 passes to shooter 2 and drives to
the net. Shooter 2 can pass back to Shooter 1 before the net, go
around the net and pass to Shooter 1, or walk out from either side.
Alternate sides.

Side "B' – Drag and shoot. Rebounders on each side of net for tips,
screens and rebounds.

Key Teaching Points (KTP)

Key Execution Points (KEP)

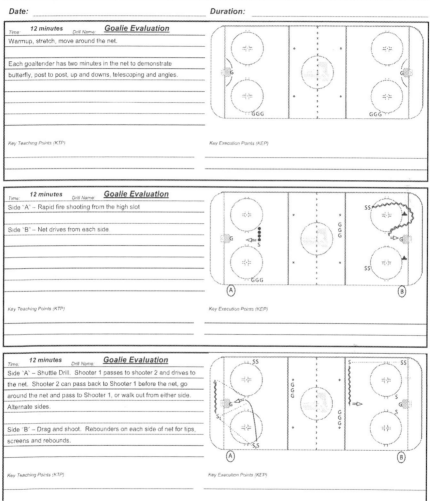

West Edmonton Wild
Goaltender Session

Date: _____   **Duration:** _____

Time: **12 minutes**   *Drill Name:* **_Goalie Evaluation_**

Side "A" – Shooter rims puck. Goalie stops the puck, passes to the shooter at the hash marks who then skates across the ice for a shot. Alternate sides.

Side "B" – Shooter skates around pylon and drives to the net for a shot. Goalie must hustle back to his net, find his angle and play the shot. Alternate sides.

Key Teaching Points (KTP)

Key Execution Points (KEP)
Goalies play each side at least twice.
Switch ends halfway through

Time: **12 minutes**   *Drill Name:* **_Goalie Evaluation_**

Side "A" – Goalie skates to the corner and makes a stretch pass to The shooter at the red line. Shooter cuts to the middle around the Pylon and then goes in on a breakaway.

Side "B" – Three shot drill. Shooter 1 from high slot, followed by Shooter 2 and then across to Shooter 3 (or Shooter 3 first and then Across to Shooter 2).

Key Teaching Points (KTP)

Key Execution Points (KEP)
Goalies play each side at least twice
Switch ends halfway through

Time: _____   *Drill Name:* _____

Key Teaching Points (KTP)

Key Execution Points (KEP)

"Dig Deep"   Page 2

Ideally, the first phase of the evaluation process will require players to demonstrate the desired set of skills. I like to use a couple of ice sessions comprised primarily of drills to accomplish this. Then, before any cuts are made, there should be some preliminary scrimmages. Why? Well, I believe that it is dangerous to make decisions based solely on drills. You should see everyone in a game-like situation. As previously mentioned, some players are great in practice and struggle once they are put in a competitive situation. Other players aren't overly impressive in practice but they are tenacious competitors. You want to make sure you don't make mistakes on those types of players. Once you've had a chance to look at everyone you should be able to split the players into three rough categories. Group one would be the "probables," group two would be the "maybes" and group three would be the "probably-nots." Group one you can set aside for a while. You won't be cutting them right away so can look at them more closely when the numbers get smaller. Group three will likely be on your first list of cuts. This will allow you to focus your attention on group two.

The second phase of the evaluation process should be to sort group two into the other categories. To do this, you should ideally refine your scrimmage groups so that those who have similar preliminary evaluation scores end up skating together (i.e. a scrimmage group for each of your three categories). After watching the group two scrimmages, it should be possible to sort the players into groups one or three. When you watch the other scrimmages it will give you the opportunity to pick out any group three players who may deserve one more chance or any group one players who aren't making the grade. There are usually a few who were initially misclassified so this will help you ensure that nobody is being missed. At the end of this phase it should be possible to cut the numbers down quite significantly and you can move forward with your group one players.

It is my opinion that this second phase of the evaluation process should be primarily scrimmage. The final deciding factor in whether or not to take a player will be to see how effective he or she is in a game situation. Therefore, you want to simulate games as closely as possible. Note that your scrimmages don't have to be ... and probably shouldn't always be ... five-on-five. Four-on-four and three-on-three scrimmages are good ways to evaluate creativity of players on offense as well as agility on defense. Two-on-two and one-on-one scrimmages in a confined area are a great way to assess speed and toughness. Five-on-four, five-on-three and four-on-three may help you spot talent in special team play. Using many different situations will allow you to develop a well rounded evaluation of each player.

The third and final phase of the evaluation process should be the actual exhibition games. Players need to turn up their intensity an extra notch once opposing teams are involved and it is easier for some players than it is for others. Those who can raise their game to another level are the ones who are going to stand out as candidates for the final team. This phase also makes it easier for a coach to look at intangibles such as hockey sense, coachability and attitude. During a game you are with the players in the dressing room and on the bench. This enables you to see these intangibles much more easily than when you are watching from the stands.

Something that I have found very helpful in gaining insight into the character of players is a player profile form. I have provided an example of one that I used recently. It is a short questionnaire that all players are required to fill out. Not only does it provide me with some information that will help me get to know players better but it also assists me in determining what kind of attitude they have. Someone who takes pride in doing a good job and thoughtfully answers each question is quite likely a better team player than one who approaches the task carelessly.

Player Profile Form

 # WEST EDMONTON WILD

Player Profile

Name: _____

Nickname: _____

Shot: (Right or Left) _____

Position: – Please be specific and list preferences in order – (i.e. 1. Center, 2. Right Wing, 3. Left Wing or 1. Left Defence, 2. Right Defence) we realize that most forwards can play all three positions and most D-men can play left or right but we would like to have your preferences.

_____

Our motto this year is "**Dig Deep**"

1. Give us an example of when you had to "dig deep" as a hockey player in order to help your team.

_____
_____
_____

List 3 strengths that you would bring to the West Edmonton Wild:

1. _____
2. _____
3. _____

What would be some good team goals that the Wild could use at the Alberta Cup?

_____
_____
_____
_____

If you were selected for the team, what individual goals would you set?

_____
_____
_____
_____

Body language is another factor that I watch very closely. A player who expresses frustration or quits too easily should obviously raise a red flag. One who attempts to rally his or her team mates and plays more tenaciuosly in the face of adversity is one who likely has the type of attitude you are looking for.

So how many evaluators should be involved in the process? Well, you want to have enough so that you lessen the probability of missing anything. On the other hand, if you have too many then there are so many opinions that it is difficult to sort through them all. I would suggest that during the first phase, it is a good idea to have as many good people as possible. Nine or ten for every hundred players would be a pretty good guideline. During the second phase you could safely cut the number by at least half because chances are you would only be looking seriously at twenty five to forty players at this point. During the third phase it is usually just the coaching staff that would still be evaluating although involving additional experts in key areas like defence and goaltending would be helpful and advisable.

How did I arrive at those numbers? Well truthfully I would say that it was trial and error. A few years ago, I was coaching a Hockey Alberta team that required me to choose a team from two hundred hopeful players over a three day period. We had seven evaluators whose endurance was tested to the max as they tried to get the job done. I had a lot of questions as we finalized the team, feeling like there were things that were being missed. All things considered, I thought that we did a pretty good job but it was much more stressful than it should have been and once we got to the competition it was clear to see that we ended up with at least three players who didn't belong. Also, inevitably, I heard about a few that we should have taken.

I went through another evaluation process the following year with only ninety hopeful players and ten evaluators. Some players picked out by individual evaluators during the process initially met with some resistance in the evaluation group but because we weren't as rushed, we had time to take another look at those players and in the end, some eventually made the team. Overall, I thought that we did a very thorough job and I felt much more confident that we had given all players a fair chance and arrived at the very best team that we could have.

Because hockey is such a fast game and there are so many players to look at, it is advisable to have your evaluators observe only one position. For example, one group could look only at the forwards, a second group would look only at the defence and a third group would focus on goaltending. This should ease pressure and result in a more thorough evaluation.

What kind of evaluation forms should you use? Well, there is no one right answer here. Some evaluators like lots of different categories and a wide range of scores ... for example a scale of one to ten. Other people are more comfortable with a narrow range ... a scale of one to five, or maybe even one to three. As long as there is consistency the scores can be accumulated and calculated and you will have a quantitative means of comparing players. I have included an example of a form that is commonly used by minor hockey teams in Alberta.

Should scores be the absolute determining factor? I would say that it is a mistake to say that. They are just a guideline. An effective process is to combine the completion of forms with a round table discussion with evaluators after each skate. As you discuss players and hear why others gave a player a higher or lower score than you did, it provides an opportunity to consider different opinions and watch for some of the characteristics of players that you may have missed.

Player Evaluation Form

West Edmonton Wild

Player Evaluation Form

Session/Game #: _____   Team: _____   Evaluator: _____

#	Pos.	Name First	Name Last	Rank 1-2-3-4-5	Comments on Performance
1	G				
30	G				
31	G				
2	D				
3	D				
4	D				
5	D				
6	D				
7	D				
8	D				
9	D				
10	F				
11	F				
12	F				
14	F				
15	F				
16	F				
17	F				
18	F				
19	F				
20	F				

Areas to key on in Comments fir F & D:
- Skating   - Puckhandling/Passing   -Intangibles
- Shooting/Scoring - Checking/Thinking Skills -Coachability
- Offensive 1-1 Skills - Defensive 1-1 Skills

Areas to key on in Comments for G:
- Skating   - Lateral Movements   - Balance & Agility
- Positioning / Angles - Use of Hands/Feet/Stick - Rebound Control
- Passing Skills   - Consistency/Big Save   - Anticipation
- Net Coverage   - Attitude/Mental Toughness - "Stop the Puck"

Rank the top 4 Defense:
1. _____
2. _____
3. _____
4. _____

Rank the top 5 Forwards:
1. _____
2. _____
3. _____
4. _____
5. _____

Rank the Top 6 Players overall (include Goalies):
1. _____
2. _____
3. _____
4. _____
5. _____
6. _____

On the form or on an accompanying sheet, you should provide a summary reminder of skills that evaluators need to be looking for. Of course, as we discussed earlier, there are many fine skills within each category and ideally the evaluators will be given an instructional session so they understand clearly what they should be looking for. On the other hand, it is important to not get too hung up on details. Finding that

36

precise number to attach to each of a player's skills is very difficult when you are watching many players for a short period of time. You need to have one number for each player so that you can tabulate scores and compare accurately with other players. If you spend too much time refining your score, you may have enough time to get an adequate look at everyone. What I usually suggest is that you start with the assumption that every player is average and then increase or decrease that score as the session proceeds based on the specific skills that they demonstrate.

When the forms are complete and you are sitting around the table with your evaluators, it is important to establish the right environment for making good decisions. Everyone sees the game a bit differently and there are lots of different opinions that can and should come out. If you have evaluation group members with strong personalities, they may overwhelm the discussion and the ideas of the less vocal group members may be suppressed. Establishing a process that gives every person a fair opportunity to speak will reduce the chance that something will be missed.

As you refine your team and make final selections there are a few additional considerations to keep in mind. Ensuring that you don't have only one type of player was mentioned earlier. If, for example, you are getting out-muscled in exhibition games then you are likely going to need more size and strength. If you are having trouble scoring goals, you will need to take a close look at all of the skilled players who are available. One suggestion that I would have is to challenge your team with strong opponents as much as possible during the exhibition season. I remember one season in Bantam AAA we went through the evaluation process and chose a team with as much skill as I had ever seen at that level. After a few exhibition games we looked unstoppable and the skilled players seemed to have little difficulty dealing with the physical play of opponents. The problem was that we were testing ourselves against mediocre teams. It wasn't until we finalized the team and came up against bigger and tougher opponents that we realized that we couldn't compete physically. Unfortunately the final decisions had been made and we struggled with that part of our game all season.

As coaches we are all aware of the necessary components for a championship team. Make sure that you look for them as you are fine tuning the team. Do you have a power play quarterback? Are there fearless, quick and hard working players who will be good at killing penalties? Do you have players who can win face-offs? Do you have anyone who is willing to step up and make the big hit? Create a list for yourself and see if you can check off all of the components before you finalize your selections.

An extremely important ingredient for a successful team (many would say the most important ingredient) is great goaltending. With that in mind, I find it amazing how many coaches will make decisions on this position with little or no expertise. If you have any questions at all, I would strongly recommend that you bring in someone who knows the position well. If there isn't a goaltender coach or goaltender expert who you are familiar with then check for goaltending coaches in the phone book. It may cost you a few dollars but it will, in all likelihood, be money well spent!

Again I can relate a story that illustrates my point. As we got down to the last few goalies during an evaluation of our Bantam AAA team one year, there was one young fellow who had amazing tenacity, great athletic ability and was making amazing save after amazing save in the scrimmages and exhibition games. Despite the fact that he had previously played in a very low tier and had seemingly come out of nowhere, he continued to impress us. Although we didn't have a goaltender coach on staff, we all were quite certain that he would be a good choice as the backup goaltender and so we made the decision to keep him. It was a big mistake! Once the regular season started it seemed that any time we put him into a game he froze up because he lacked the confidence to play at that level and his decision making, especially while playing the puck, was extremely poor and it put us in some very tough positions defensively. The problem was that we were so caught up in his ability to make spectacular saves that we missed the whole picture. A more competent goaltender evaluator would have picked out those shortcomings and would probably have steered us in a different direction.

Evaluating defencemen can also be tricky. A good defenceman, especially a steady stay-at-home kind of player, will do some subtle things that untrained evaluators may have trouble picking out. It is easy to spot the offensive minded guy who gets the blistering shot on net or joins the rush to create a great scoring chance but how about the guy who just does an effective job of playing tough and eliminating opposition chances around his net? This is the kind of guy that you are going to want out on the ice in the last minute of a tough game when you are protecting a lead but maybe this kind of guy isn't going to stand out in lower intensity scrimmages and exhibition games. Again the solution is to ensure that there is enough expertise on your coaching staff and with your evaluators. Asking specific questions may help your evaluators to focus on these subtle but important things. For example, "In the last minute of a game, which of the defencemen that we have in camp would you want out there?"

So hopefully you have been able to establish a process that identifies the players who possess the skills that you are looking for and who can play the roles that you identify as important. Is that all you need to consider? Not quite. There is one very important component that we haven't discussed yet and that is chemistry. You don't have to look further than the New York Rangers in the last few years of the old NHL collective bargaining agreement (prior to the player's strike of 2004-2005) to see a good example of a team that had all the talent in the world but lacked the chemistry to be successful. Every summer you would read newspaper stories about the superstars that the Rangers were signing to lucrative long-term contracts and you would think "OK, this is the year that they finally put it all together!" But year after year the team would underachieve and miss the playoffs. Why was that? Well it wasn't lack of talent so it had to be that they just didn't have the right chemistry.

Another attribute of a defenceman that is extremely valuable, is the ability to make a good pass out of the defensive zone to initiate a breakout. This skill can be easily missed by evaluators but it should be an important area of focus. If a player is struggling with the pass in a tryout environment, when there is no structure to the opposition's forecheck, then he or she will really be in trouble as the season progresses and passing options are limited. When you think about it ... it really doesn't matter how talented your forwards are if the defencemen on your team can't get them the puck!

So how do you create this elusive chemistry? It is a question that is not easy to answer. The Rangers put together a bunch of talented players who all were highly motivated to win a Stanley Cup but that didn't seem to work. Some believe that putting a bunch of great friends together will create the perfect team ... but often this creates a "country club" sort of environment and the work ethic isn't sufficient to get the job done. During the playoffs of the 2003 – 2004 NHL season, Darryl Sutter put together a hard working bunch of mostly unknown players who almost brought the Cup home for the Calgary Flames. Had they found the right formula? Certainly they had a strong follow up season in 2005 – 2006 but once they hit the playoffs, they just couldn't find the same sort of magic and they lost out early.

One of the interesting theories that I have heard was discussed by Barry Smith, then an assistant coach to Scotty Bowman for the Detroit Red Wings, at the 2002 International Coaches Conference in Montreal. He believed that you need to have strong leaders on a team but if there are too many, it will create conflict. Those who want to lead will be frustrated because they aren't able to fill a role that is significant enough to be satisfying. So you start with a small but effective leadership team that you can count on. You will also have a number of players who will play hard and sacrifice for the team no matter what the situation is. These energetic guys are able to lift a team with their impressive work ethic and physical play. Often their skill level isn't extremely high but they are consistent and predictable. In the middle you have the more skilled players who can be either a positive or a negative force depending on the situation. If they are happy with their role, they will move the team in a positive direction. If they are unhappy, they will be a negative force. It is these guys who can make or break the team chemistry. If there are too many of them and they feel like they are being underutilized, then they can create a very negative environment that turns the team in the wrong direction. If they can all fill roles that are satisfying to them and beneficial to the team, then you will likely have the right components for good chemistry.

Here is where your homework can really come in handy! If you are making final team selections and you are looking at two players for the final spot. Player one is a skilled player who may not be given a significant role on the team and has a reputation of being a demanding player. Player two is an energetic guy who isn't nearly as talented as player one but is willing to do anything for the team. Who do you take? Well, unless there is a particular role available to fit the capabilities of the skilled player, you would probably lean towards player two. That way it is less likely that potential negative reactions of the first player will come out due to dissatisfaction about his or her role on the team and have a detrimental effect on the team chemistry.

Here are some other thoughts about evaluation, selection and team chemistry from some great names in coaching:

"I've got 18 skaters in there. Six like me and six don't like me. My job as a coach is to keep the six who don't give a damn away from the six who don't like me"

- Fred Shero, Hockey Coach

"A deep thinker has a great understanding of the game of hockey. He is someone who has to have most things mapped out and needs an understanding of why we do things. He's got to sort through it in his mind and it's got to make sense for him to do it. Then you've got the player at the other end of the spectrum, the blood and guts type player who has no thought, just knows how to play hard. You need both kinds to be successful"

- Marc Crawford, Hockey Coach*

"There are two types of people in life. There are people who are afraid to fail and there are people who are afraid to succeed. I want to be around the people who are afraid to fail"

- Brian Sutter, Hockey Coach*

"Every team has soft players (those who pick which team they want to compete against ... they don't compete every night). It's up to the coach to determine who the soft players are. You hope that you don't have more than two or three because then you are not going to win"

- Jacques Demers, Hockey Coach*

"Being simplistic, there are givers and there are takers; a team needs givers. Contrast the basketball careers of Bill Russell and Kareem Abdul Jabar. Bill Russell won 11 NBA championships with the Boston Celtics, whereas Kareem Abdul Jabar, who was the pre-eminent offensive NBA player in the same era, did not win any. Bill Russell took pride in making others better; Kareem Abdul Jabar never used his gift to make teammates successful"

- George Kingston, Hockey Coach*

"I've always believed that you have to have a minimum of seven strong leaders on your team. The way that life works, there are going to be certain days that someone may not be as capable of leading as he would like to be. You've got to have other people ready to step in"

- Andy Murray, Hockey Coach*

"I have coached for a long time, and I have always seen two categories of players. There are the carriers and there are guys who have to be carried. I have always tried to surround myself with more carriers. If you have too many guys who need to be carried, you are in for a long darn season"

- Dave King, Hockey Coach*

"On a really good team the role players ... the foot soldiers ... stand out to me. You can't have enough of them. I've always felt the most important thing is to have role players who accept their role. Role players are the most important component of good teams"

- Scotty Bowman, Hockey Coach*

So what is the magic formula? Well there are lots of interesting theories and each individual will need to decide whether to use them, modify them, or discard them and come up with something unique. My objective is to simply raise a few questions that you may want to think about as you proceed through your evaluation. It will be important for you as a coach to establish a process that you are comfortable with and it will likely be continually refined over time.

The final step of the evaluation process, and it is an uncomfortable one, is releasing the players who don't make the team. It is something that I have always had a difficult time with so I don't know if I am the best one to be giving advice about it. On the other hand, I have been a keen observer of how others handle the situation because of my quest to find a process that I am comfortable with. In addition to that, I have made many mistakes when releasing players through the years and while I don't feel very good about them, I believe that I have learned from them! In any case, I believe that I have improved my approach although I am sure that it will never be easy for me.

Making the first round of cuts is always a bit easier because there are usually large numbers of players who are trying out for the team and are just there for the experience … they don't realistically expect to make it. Sure, there is always some hope … they wouldn't be there if there wasn't at least a slim chance … but it is rare with these players that the news about being released meets with any great shock. At this point in the process, you can probably get away with posting the list of players who are moving on to the next phase of the tryouts or perhaps you can tell the players that they will receive a phone call if they are going move on. I would usually have a good talk to each group of players at the end of the last tryout session prior to cuts and thank them for their participation. Having something nice to say about the caliber of players at the tryout and acknowledging that everyone put in a very good effort will at least serve to ensure that the players who don't make it are walking away with a good feeling about themselves.

As you get closer to the final team, it gets more and more difficult to give a player the bad news. At that point in the process, players expect to be on the team and often the dreams of many years are shattered when they are released. So is there any easy way to release a player? I would say no … and hopefully, it is something that you never feel good about. On the other hand, for the player's sake I think that there are some suggestions to consider.

First of all, I believe that it is best to give the message face to face. Using less personal means of communication like posting a list or even making a phone call doesn't give you an opportunity to gauge the player's reaction and respond to it. There may be some questions that are unanswered and for the player to walk away without having as much information as possible about the decision is unfair and could be very damaging to their confidence and future development. Many times there won't be any questions but in a face to face situation, people feel better about at least having the opportunity to ask. It also may establish trust and good rapport so if there are future questions, the player may be more comfortable asking them.

A second suggestion would be to keep the message very brief and direct. Something like … "It has been a very competitive tryout and you played very well but I'm sorry to tell you that you won't be on the team this season. Do you have any questions?" At that point the ball is in the player's court. If there are questions, they can be asked. If not, the player can make a hasty exit … and I would suggest that this is the most likely scenario. One of my colleagues once suggested to me that once someone hears the bad news, you can go on talking for half an hour and chances are he or she won't remember a word that you say. I believe that there is a lot of truth in that. I used to go on and on about all of the great qualities, the bright future and possible opportunities with our team next season that the player might have but at the end of the day, I never felt like he or she felt any better about the situation. Most of the time as I was talking, I sensed that the individual couldn't wait for me to finish so a quick exit could be made!

I'm not suggesting that you don't give positive feedback but I just think that there is a better time and place for it. Inviting questions or giving the player your number for a future call could be one way to provide the feedback. Another good idea that I witnessed at a junior A camp was to give the player a brief report card with a few feedback comments that could be reviewed at a better time. Of course if it is a player that you are hoping to keep in touch with as a prospect for the team in the future, it won't be long before contact is made, their progress is discussed, and feedback is provided as part of the next season's recruiting process.

A final suggestion that I would have is to finish with eye contact, a hearty handshake, thanks for trying out, and best wishes for the future. This reinforces the fact that hockey is just a game and this decision shouldn't have any impact on future friendship with the player. It is unfortunate when a cut is the last word that is ever spoken between coach and player. It would be great if the smile and greeting that I get the day after a cut is exactly the same as the one the day before but unfortunately, it has never happened. I guess that would be a lot to ask! But I do think that after the initial shock, my contact with players who I'd had a good sincere meeting with as I released them has been quite positive. Similarly, it seems that there have been more hard feelings when I have been unhappy with my approach to releasing a player.

My own personal experience is that as I've refined my process, I have had fewer sleepless nights at this time of year. What hasn't changed, however, is the feeling of satisfaction and relief that I've experienced when it is all over. Those feelings progress to excitement and anticipation when the team is in place and we can start final preparations for the season to begin.

Chapter 3
The Practice

"We are what we repeatedly do.
Excellence, then, is not an act
but a habit"

- Aristotle

So the team is chosen and it is now time to begin the ongoing process of trying to become the best that you can be. I'm sure that most coaches would agree that practice time is the most important time for teams interested in a successful season. It doesn't really matter who is on the team. If it isn't prepared, the chances of success aren't great.

Setting a practice schedule for the year is your first consideration. As discussed in the first chapter, it is something that should be considered when preparing the seasonal plan. Chances are that it will be adjusted as the season wears on but it is important to have a starting point. First of all, you want to decide how many practices you want per week and then you can arrange the optimal time and location. Deciding on the theme of the practices at different points of the schedule is the next consideration. Personally, I like to establish my conditioning and defensive strategy very early in the season and then work on other aspects of the game. Others may follow a different approach.

Part of the planning process is to identify important competitions of the season. Playoffs, of course, are a main focus and there will likely be some major tournaments. You need to do what you can to ensure that players are as well prepared as possible at those times. Preparation of on ice strategies and tactics is very important but you also have to consider physical and mental preparation. I have heard this called "energy management." If players are mentally and physically tired when they go into these competitions their chances of success will be reduced. At one coaching conference that I attended I was quite surprised to hear Perry Pearn, then an assistant coach for the New York Rangers, say that it is unusual for an NHL team to practice for longer than 45 minutes per day for the last part of the season. They recognize what a long grind the regular season is and they want to ensure that players are as mentally and physically fresh as possible going into the playoffs. Once the overall practice schedule and strategy is set, it needs to be communicated to the players so they will know what to expect as the season unfolds.

On the ice, it is important to set rules and guidelines for the players as early as possible. I do it at my first practice session. My first basic rule is that the whistle means that players immediately stop what they are doing and rush in to where I am standing. The last person in will always skate a lap. This may seem a little harsh but I have found that it creates a bit of a friendly competition as players try to avoid that extra lap and if they are getting to the whiteboard quickly, it cuts down on wasted time between drills. Another rule that I like to establish is that everything is done at the speed and intensity of a game. My assistants and I are always reminding the players that they will play as they practice. Full speed and 100% effort in practice will translate into good game performance.

A third rule that I believe is very important to establish is the need for active observation. This is a term I first heard many years ago at a University of Alberta Golden Bears hockey camp. I was a young participant at the camp and Clare Drake was our instructor. Active observation occurs when your players watch others closely as they participate in drills. When they do that they not only have the opportunity to learn new tactics and strategies, but they will be more ready and sharper mentally when it is their turn. If you observe minor hockey games and practices, you will sometimes see players pushing, shoving and joking around as they wait on the bench or in line. While they are doing this, they are obviously not watching what their teammates are doing on the ice. Surprisingly, it is a habit that can follow a player for many years. I have had some players on my junior team who, during the game, will sit on the player's bench without observing what is happening on the ice. I will always step in and say something about it. Although I am not aware of any studies to prove it, I would wager that there is a strong correlation between poor observation skills and lack of success.

"You can observe a lot by just watching"

- Yogi Berra, Baseball Manager

When planning your individual practices, there are some important components to consider. *Conditioning*, of course, is of major importance and it should be integrated into drills as much as possible ... especially if your practice time is limited. Sometimes a drill has no other purpose. Sure you can work on fitness with off-ice activities, and we will talk more about that, but there is no substitute for a good hard skate! *Introducing and refining skills and tactics* should always take up a lot of your practice time, especially for the younger players. We will talk about integrating those into other drills but sometimes monotonous repetition is the best way to learn quickly. For example, one of the things that I used to require when I was coaching young players was twenty five backhand shots against the boards when they first got onto the ice ... before they were allowed to join the pre-practice shinny game.

"We did believe in the "agony of repetition." We had good variety in our practice drills because I think we introduced new things when they came along, but we spent a lot of time on the basics and we strove for quality of execution. That's one of the things we talked about with the players, that we didn't want to try 101 different things, but the ones we wanted to do we wanted to do well"

- Clare Drake, Hockey Coach*

Because hockey is a team game, *systems* are also very important and how much practice time they take up will depend on whether they are very basic or more complex. You usually you won't get into much of this until the players are a bit older. It may overload your players and take up too much ice time to practice all of your systems right away but you want to accomplish it as early in the season as possible. As discussed in the first chapter, a strategy and a timeline is a good idea. Because offensive systems usually come more naturally to players than defensive systems I like to start with defensive zone coverage. Players can usually survive on their offensive instincts for a while before you have to get too organized. Eventually, you will add other systems such as the fore check, the breakout, the power play, the penalty kill, regroups and face offs. Of course there will be some other strategies to be used at different times during a game (last minute strategies when the goaltender is out, for example) and you will also need to build them into your teaching schedule.

Many teams use manuals to outline systems for their players and they can supplement the teaching that is done in practice, with team meetings and during dry land activities. One approach that I have tried recently is having players draw out the systems on paper as they are learning them. This is a technique that may be helpful for learners who are more visual, or those who need to do something active to supplement their reading.

Another important part of the practice that sometimes gets neglected is the *competitive* portion. Playing hockey involves a series of battles and races and you want your players to be as hungry as possible when they are involved in those situations. Also, players love a competition so adding an incentive to a battling drill will often help to turn up the intensity. It's amazing what extent some players will go to win those little games!

This brings me to the final component of a practice, and it may be the most important one ... *fun!* Players have to enjoy coming to the rink. If they don't and the players lose their desire to play, all of the planning that you have done may end up being a waste of time.

Ideally most of the fun will be on the ice but during a long season and there will be times when players will wish that they were doing something other than practicing. Coaches need to be creative in finding something different. Maybe a pizza night or team breakfast after a practice ... or a team activity like a movie or another sporting activity. One thing that I always look for is the opportunity to get out on the outdoor ice. Something about getting out in the fresh air energizes the players and takes them to a new level of enjoyment.

"Be consistent with what you do in practice. Repetition is the key, but not boring repetition. Have fun doing it. I really didn't believe in one-and-a-half-hour practices. I believe in a fast-paced 45 minutes to an hour. To the point, do it, do it well, go out, see you later. I love tempo. I love a transition tempo team. If you get a team to practice with tempo, you're going to form good habits"

- Jacques Demers, Hockey Coach*

We've talked about the desirable components of practice and drill selection is, of course, very important. In addition to that, here are some other general considerations that may help:

- *Provide some variety but don't go overboard!* I heard Mike Johnson telling the delegates at a recent coaching conference that the "80% rule" is a good one to keep in mind. Studies have shown that 80% of the drills should be ones that the players have seen before and only 20% should be new. Most players like a bit of variety but they also like a lot of familiarity. Variety keeps the practice interesting ... it requires players to be mentally sharp. Familiarity provides the opportunity for a challenge ... to hopefully improve on previous performance.

- *Be as game specific as possible.* Players should be practicing what they are likely to be doing in a game situation. Analyze your drills and use your imagination to think of improvements. Would a back checker make it more game like? How about adding a pass? Can the coaches get involved to challenge the players as they skate through the drill?

- *Encourage good habits.* These are things that you would want to see during a game and so it only makes sense to practice them! I talked earlier about the importance of doing things at game speed. Here are some other examples:
  - If a puck is lost during a drill, ensure that the player stops to pick it up rather than continuing in hopes of grabbing another loose puck. You may temporarily lose a bit of flow but your players will get into the habit of never giving up on the puck.
  - Ensure the drill doesn't end once the shot on goal is taken. Have your players stop in front of the net for a potential rebound or, if the puck is deflected away from the net, ensure that they jump to pursue it right away.
  - Practice shooting in stride. Players often get lazy during shooting drills. They slow down, coast and wind up for the big shot. Chances are they will never do that in a game situation. There won't be time. Shooting in stride is an effective skill that gives goaltenders headaches. They never quite know when the shot is coming!
  - Practice transition. Sometimes, during a shooting drill, I will require players to skate hard back to the blue line every time they take their shot on goal. This underlines the importance of always keeping defensive responsibilities in mind. During a game, a turnover will often require that sort of a quick reaction on the part of players.
  - Take away time and space. During practice, players can challenge quickly and aggressively without the fear of being scored on. Sure they will get beaten from time to time but a practice is the time to take chances ... when the risk is low. As players experience success they will gain skill and confidence. Over time your team's puck pressure during games will show a big improvement.
  - Encourage teammates to be tough on one another. Players aren't doing a teammate any favours by taking it easy on him or her during a practice. They aren't going to get that treatment by opponents during a game! It will help everyone get better if you insist on finished checks, strength with their sticks and game-like competition!

- *Involve your goaltender.* Even with all of the coaching material that has been published to encourage goaltender involvement, I very rarely watch a practice where they are involved as much as they should be. Most coaches will tell you that goaltenders represent the most important position on the team so it doesn't make sense that they are often taken for granted and underutilized. There are a few things that you could consider to improve the situation.
  - Add extra shots. With many drills there is an opportunity to add additional shots for goaltenders to play. Use your assistant coaches to spot extra pucks for this.
  - Play it out. This was discussed previously from the shooters point of view but it is even more important for the goaltender. Don't end the drill with a shot that gets kicked out into the slot or off to the corner. Have your shooters pursue rebounds and continue the play. This encourages the goaltender to never lose focus or give up on the puck.
  - Have your goaltender play the puck. An extremely important attribute of the top goaltenders these days is their ability to play the

puck. Some are so good at it that they are like a third defenceman in the defensive zone. If it is such an important skill, goalies should have the opportunity to practice it yet I rarely see it integrated into a drill.

- *Encourage communication.* Coaches at any level will likely tell you that their team doesn't communicate enough. Remember that players will play as they practice. If they aren't getting used to communicating on the ice during practice, they won't do it in a game. Calling for passes is just part of the equation. Talk to your players about what instructions they can provide for teammates to help them out in a game situation and then ensure that they use them in practice. This is another area that you can work with your goaltenders on as well. If you watch top goalies, they are always shouting instructions to teammates to help them out.

- *Rotate positions.* Why is it always the forwards who are the puck carriers during a one-on-one drill? Don't defencemen ever need to beat someone one-on-one to advance the puck? Don't forwards ever have to know how to play a one-on-one situation as the last man back? Make sure that you allocate some time for players to learn skills from the defensive side as well as the offensive side of the puck!

- *Add-in skills.* As I mentioned, the practices of younger players should be heavily laden with skill development. When players progress, there is more emphasis on other areas but the need to learn and practice skills is there at all levels. Adding a skill … like a pivot here or a fake shot there … to an established drill can provide more opportunity for a player to improve. Certain skills may require extra attention. The backhand shot, for example, will rarely be used in practice if your instruction to the players is to simply take a shot. It will probably be necessary to require a backhand if you want your players to practice it. I remember watching a 3-2 game in the Hurricanes / Oilers Stanley Cup final where the Oilers scored two of their three goals on the backhand and the third was on a great backhand pass set up! It is a very important skill, and a difficult one to master, especially with today's curved sticks, yet it is often neglected in practice!

- *Integrate some "curve ball training."* This is a phrase that I learned from my sister Leslie Sproule who coaches synchronized swimming at the international level. To help athletes learn to deal with situations that are unexpected and potentially distracting she works through realistic problem scenarios so that they can practice adapting. There are lots of opportunities to do this during hockey practices. If you are preparing for a team that has the tendency to use certain tactics or team systems, then your practice time will be effectively used by simulating those and teaching your players how to react to them.

- *Tell them why.* I once talked to a Bantam AAA parent who told me how much he appreciated my explanation to his son about why he was doing a drill. He suggested that it was the first time that anyone had ever done it and it cleared up a bunch of confusion. This really surprised me. I just took it for granted that the reason for doing a drill was so crucial that it was always part of the set up. If you are neglecting that part of your explanation, make sure that you add it in!

- *Watch other practices.* Every time I go and watch another team practice, I walk away with new ideas. To keep your practices fresh, take the time to go and see how somebody else does it. I can guarantee that it will pay off. Even better, see if the coach has a few minutes after the practice to explain to you what he is doing and why. The team that I get out to watch most often because they are close to me is the University of Alberta Golden Bears. Watching this great team go through their paces is a learning experience in itself and the coaches have always been very generous with me when I have called to ask them questions about their approach.

- *Involve your assistants.* In your pre-season planning, you probably spent a lot of time deciding who you wanted to work with. Hopefully you chose people who will add knowledge and experience to the team. Make sure that you take advantage of that during practices. Part of your practice plan should be to consider how you can make optimal use of this valuable resource.

- *Finish the practice with a few words about what the team can expect next.* Next on the team's agenda there will often be a big game, or maybe it will just be the next practice. Either way, leaving the players with a few words is a very good way to start their mental preparation for the next visit to the rink.

So far we have discussed on-ice practices and obviously they are crucial to the success of the team. Ice time is a scarce resource, however, and no matter how much you have scheduled it will probably not be enough to get through everything that you want to cover. Effective planning of off-ice time can be helpful as a supplement. Here are some suggestions:

- *Pre-ice your team prior to practice sessions.* If you are able to quickly explain drills prior to hitting the ice you will require less time for that during the practice. This will translate into more time for players to actually participate. Another possibility is to post your drills on the dressing room wall for your players to review.

- *Have players stretch off-ice.* The few minutes that players use at the beginning and end of practices is important for warming up / cooling down the body. However, it is something that can be done in any open space. Maybe your practice arena has a suitable open area?

- *Use a gymnasium or a field to work through your systems.* Often when you are discussing these, or doing a preliminary walk-through there is a lot of standing around. Why not stand around off the ice when time is not as scarce ... or costly!?

- *Do a lot of your conditioning off-ice.* Jogging, swimming and biking are examples of great cardio-vascular activities. Strength and flexibility are also important areas of conditioning that you can't work on much during your ice time. Putting together regular off-ice training sessions can be very beneficial to your team.

- *Add in some mental training.* This is another thing that is difficult to work on during on-ice practices. As discussed previously, more and more teams are employing the services of sports psychologists to help with this important area. Some use chaplains to help the players with some spiritual guidance.

- *Make sure to add in ample time for rest and reflection.* During our discussions of planning, we have talked about many on and off ice strategies that can be used to build your team. All can be extremely beneficial but beware of overload! Additional practice time is of no benefit to players who are mentally and/or physically exhausted. They will have difficulty retaining any information that you want to get across. Sometimes the best thing that you can do for your team is simply give them a little time off.

Another great benefit of off-ice activities is that they promote team chemistry. Players get a chance to know each other better and the team becomes more cohesive. My son Sean told me that his junior team, the Medicine Hat Tigers, regularly went swimming together. They all looked forward to the outings as good fun and a great change of pace. Another interesting comment that he made was that these well conditioned athletes were always just exhausted after the swimming sessions. Thinking about it, I imagine that it was because they were using a lot of different muscles that they didn't get a chance to work on while playing hockey. I'm sure that this had a very positive effect on their overall level of fitness.

The selection of actual drills that the team will use will vary from coach to coach. To accumulate ideas you may want to dialogue with other coaches, observe practices or go to one of the many great drill books that are available. Over time you should come up with a set of "core drills" that the players will see regularly throughout the season. These should cover the critical skills, tactics and systems that you identify. Periodically, you can bring in new drills or make some modifications to your core drills to give the players a bit of a fresh look and a new challenge.

Over the following pages, I will outline the core drills that I am presently using. Note that I am always refining this set and so it will change slightly from season to season. Also, there will be some variation depending on the age group of the players that you are coaching. Surprisingly, however, with the exception of additional systems work for the older players, I have found that my drills haven't varied too much from one age group to the next. I have had questions about whether some of my drills were too difficult for younger players but I have found that if explained well, they respond favourably to the challenge.

For each drill, I will provide a diagram and some commentary about exactly what the player and/or team is practicing and what some of the key teaching points are. You may very well recognize the drill or know it under a different name. This isn't surprising because many of these have been around for a while and things change as they get passed from coach to coach. Whatever you want to call the drill, make sure your players know the name so they can recognize it easily when they are reviewing the practice schedule. You may want to provide each player with a drill book that they can carry with them and perhaps get a chance to study each drill more closely.

Skating Drills

These are an important part of every coach's repertoire. When I was coaching younger players, a significant portion of every practice was for power skating ... drills with no pucks that worked specifically on key areas (forward, backward, pivots, stopping, tight turns, crossovers, etc.). With older players I tend to integrate most of my skating into puck-carrying and shooting drills. Of course there are times to throw in a few good old fashioned skating drills. Team conditioning may need to be tuned up or you may need to get the attention of players ... when unruly at practice or perhaps after a bad game, for example! In any case, there are many good power skating books that outline a variety of drills. Most are quite simple and you can certainly improvise and provide variety. Here are a few basic ones that I use.

Stops and starts – This drill focuses on acceleration and proper stopping technique. I generally split the team into groups of six or seven and have them skate end to end one group after the other ... stopping and accelerating in the opposite direction each time they hear the whistle. Ensure that players practice using both sides by having them face in the same direction each time they stop.

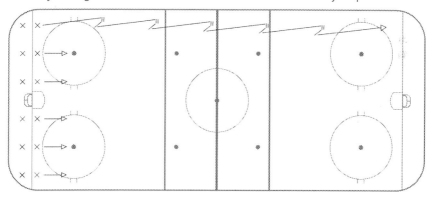

Circles – This drill focuses on forward and backward crossovers. Complete the course using just forward or just backward skating or you can require the players to always be facing in one direction so that forward to backward and backward to forward pivots are required. Make sure players complete at least one full rotation at each circle. For older players this is a good one to leave until the end of practice. The skate blades tend to create big ruts in the ice.

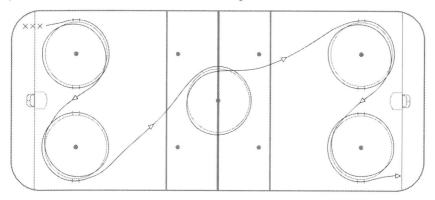

Half Circles – This focuses on the same skills as circles but it allows for players to execute at a higher speed. I quite often add pucks to this drill, especially when doing it backwards. It provides a good challenge for backwards puck carrying without the bottlenecks that arise if you try to integrate pucks with full circles.

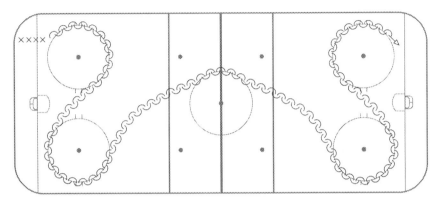

Dot to dot skating – This drill focuses on tight turns. Players work their way up the ice turning at each dot. It can be done forward, backward or alternating between the two to work on pivots.

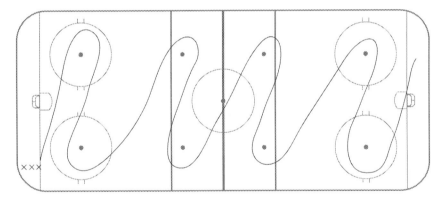

Narrow / Wide race for the puck – This is a great competitive drill that allows players to work on their acceleration and speed. On the whistle, players sprint to the far end, hoping to reach the puck ahead of their teammate so that they can get a shot away. Ensure that it is clear which side goes narrow and which goes wide!

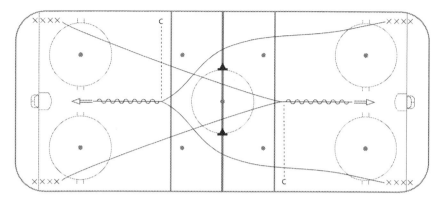

Primeau agility drill – This drill combines lateral crossovers and pivots. It works on quick feet and side to side, back to front agility. Ensure that players have an opportunity to pivot in each direction.

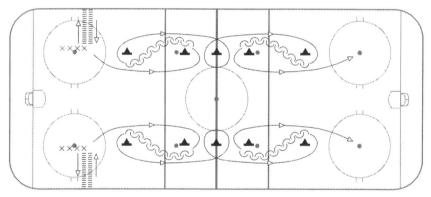

Instructions: Players in each line start by making lateral crossovers to the near boards and back ... facing up ice. They then skate on the inside of the ice to the second pylon where they pivot front to back and then back to front while they are completing a figure eight. After completion, they work their way up the ice while completing the pattern that is illustrated.

Warm-up Drills

I generally use these early in practice to warm up and create a good practice tempo. You may also insert them at other times during the practice whenever you feel that the energy level needs to be increased. By being creative and adding skills and tactics to the drills you can promote development in those key areas.

Swiss Passing Drill – This drill gives the players an opportunity to warm up in a lot of areas so I use it early in practice. Quick acceleration, quick passing and receiving followed by a quick shot is required so it has the effect of jump starting the flow of the practice. It is also a great drill for working on timing. A variation that I often use is to require a pass off the boards. Ensure that passers are moving with the puck and when they become pass receivers they should present a target, get eye contact with the passer and communicate!

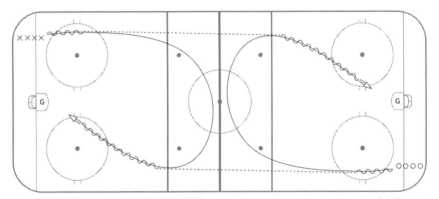

Instructions: X1 begins skating and cuts across the ice at centre. O1 begins skating, makes the pass to X1 and then cuts across at centre for a pass from X2. Upon receiving the pass, the player proceeds in for a shot on goal. The drill flows as it proceeds from side to side.

Swedish Agility Drill – This drill uses a lot of quick touch passing finishing off with a game-specific give-and-go pass and a quick shot. It is a very good drill to promote agility and quick puck movement.

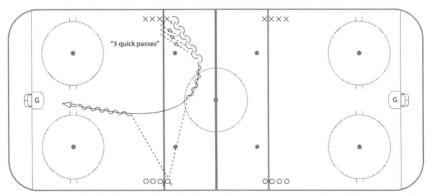

Instructions: X1 begins skating backwards, receives a pass from X2, returns the puck to X2 and then gets another pass (three quick passes). X1 then pivots,

makes a give-and-go pass to O1 and proceeds in for a shot on goal. O1 then starts the sequence in the other direction.

Shoot and Crash – This is a great drill to emphasize going to the net, a tactic that almost always creates scoring chances. The player at the net is then required to tip, screen and pick up loose rebounds. The shooter practices a quick drag and shot from either side and must place the shot strategically for his or her teammate. It is also a very good drill for goaltender awareness.

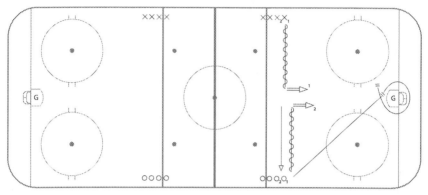

Instructions: X1 drags the puck to the middle for a shot while O1 goes hard to the net from the other side for a tip, rebound or screen. X1 then sprints to the other side of the ice where he picks up another puck for a drag and shot. O1 skates around behind the net and then back out front for another tip, rebound or screen. The next sequence starts with O2 dragging and shooting while X2 crashes the net. Players alternate sides with each turn.

Shuttle Drill – The quick give-and-go required of this drill practices tactics that you will see frequently when the offensive team attacks the net. There are different options that can be discussed and practiced. I find that it is a really good lead in to power play practice because it gets the players in a creative mindset around the net. This is a very strenuous drill for the goaltender but an excellent one as it promotes awareness of activity behind the net and forces quick movement from side to side.

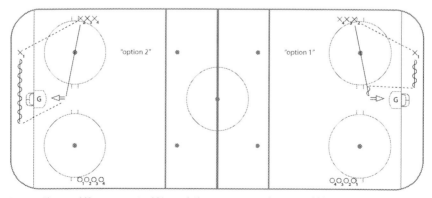

Instructions: X2 passes to X1 and then goes to the net. X1 can pass to X2 on the near side, carry around the net and pass to X2 on the other side or use X2 as

a screen or decoy and step out for a shot from either side. Once the sequence is complete, X2 goes to the corner and begins a new sequence on a pass from O1.

Long and Short Drill – This is a great drill to pick up the tempo. Players can practice open ice puck carrying with speed and you can encourage shooting in stride. For the goaltenders a quick movement across the net is required after the initial shot. To avoid collisions, make sure that it is clear which player skates the long pattern and which one is skating the short one!

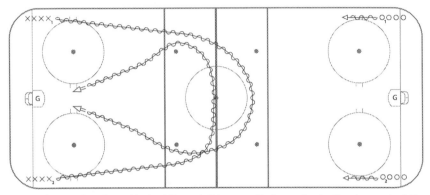

Instructions: On the whistle, X1 and O1 carry their pucks to the far end of the neutral zone (long), cross the ice and return to their zone on the other side of the ice for a shot. At the same time, X2 and O2 are carrying pucks to the near side of the neutral zone (short) where they cross and return for a shot.

Narrow and Wide Passing – A simple drill but it allows players to practice long and short passes, on their forehand and on their backhand, while simulating a high speed rush up the ice with a teammate. Players must deal with traffic through the neutral zone and must always have their heads up!

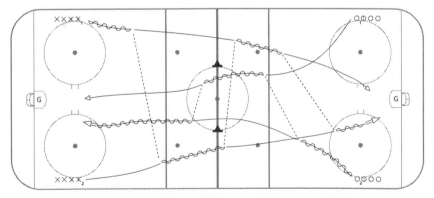

Instructions: On the whistle, O1 and O2 pass their way up the ice making sure to skate inside the pylons. X1 and X2 skate and pass in the opposite direction, making sure to go outside the pylons.

Progression: Have passers cross and drop at the far blue line and then return on the other side of the pylons (i.e. go out narrow and return wide, or out wide and return narrow)

Swift Current Agility Drill – This drill gives the players a great skate. In addition to quick acceleration and forward skating there are pivots (back to forward and forward to back) and tight turns. The player must handle a puck through the maneuvers before finishing with a shot. The goaltender will face two quick shots and will have to move quickly across the net between them.

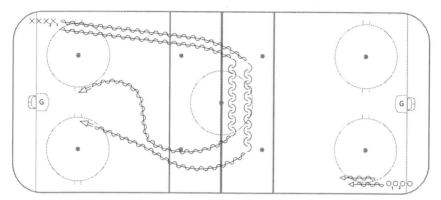

Instructions: On the whistle, X1 and X2 carry pucks to the far end of the neutral zone where they pivot forward to backwards, skate from one face-off dot to the other, and then pivot backwards to forwards prior to returning on the other side of the ice to their original zone for a shot. O1 and O2 start at the same time from the opposite end. Players should space themselves out and shoot from two different lanes as they complete the drill.

Toronto Triple – As is the case with many of my shooting drills, this drill involves a lot of skating. Some pivots are integrated and there is a pass off the boards ... a tactic that is good to practice because it can be effective in a game situation. The goaltender will face three shots in this case and must also deal with traffic in front of the net from the players who have stopped for tips or rebounds.

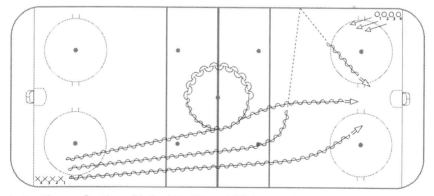

Instructions: On the whistle, X1, X2 and X3 leave with pucks. X1 drives the outside lane for a shot. X2 crosses the ice after the centre line, passes off the boards to himself and shoots from the other side of the ice. X3 skates to the circle at centre ice, pivots front to back and then back to front as he goes around the circle finishing by skating into the high slot for a shot. O1, O2 and O3 start at the same time from the opposite end of the ice.

Grizzly Weave – Lots of passing in this drill. On the way up the ice, three players will move the puck quickly as they would on a rush. On the way back they will field passes from deep in the defensive zone. Good communication is required throughout the drill. For the goaltender there will be four shots that are received in rapid succession requiring quick reactions!

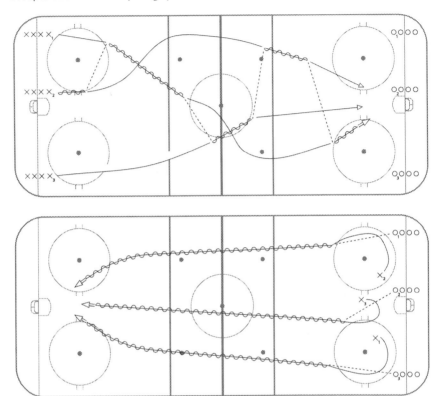

Instructions: Starting with the puck in the middle lane, X1, X2 and X3 weave up the ice, finishing with a shot on goal. They then transition and receive passes from O1, O2 and O3 as they return to their original end for shots. Players must space themselves and communicate as to who is shooting first, second and third. Once all players have passed the centre line, O1, O2 and O3 start the sequence in the other direction.

Tokyo Triple – This drill requires quick touch passing skating forward and backwards. There is also one-time shooting and a quick drag to the middle along the blue line for a shot ... very game specific! It is also quite tricky with a lot of interdependent parts and so it requires good concentration by the team.

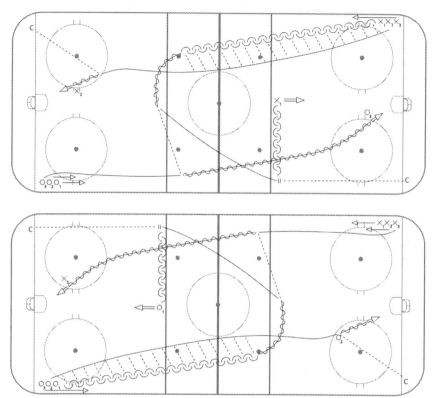

Instructions: On the first whistle X1 and X2 start up ice (O1 and O2 will start from the opposite end). X1 and O1 are skating backward while X2 and O2 are skating forward and they are making quick touch passes back and forth. As they get to the far blue line, a second whistle is blown. At that time, X2 and O2 will leave the puck and drive to the net for a pass from the coach. X1 and O1 will take the puck, drag it to the middle and look for a pass on the opposite side. There they will see X3 or O3 who will begin to sprint up the ice at the second whistle. These players go in to shoot once they receive their pass. X1 and O1 then follow up the play and set themselves in the point position to receive a final pass from the coach. They then finish the drill by dragging to the middle for a shot.

Shooting Drills are often more intense if there is more of a sense of urgency. A back-checker can provide that. Here are a couple of examples:

Boston Back-check – This drill gives a good example of inserting additional skills to enhance development. When I was first exposed to this drill, the first player would pick up a puck behind the net and just coast around until his teammate drove the net looking for a pass. Requiring three quick shots prior to retrieving the puck for a pass helps the first player develop quick shooting skills and eventually forces a quicker decision on whether to pass or shoot.

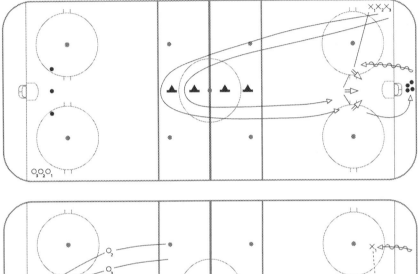

Instructions: On the whistle, X1 will sprint to the front of the net where he takes three quick shots on goal. He then goes behind the net to retrieve a puck and carries it up the side of the ice looking to pass. At the same time, X2 will skate around the far pylon and return to the zone calling for a pass. X3 is the back-checker and must try to get the inside position on X2. X1 will have the option of completing the pass to X2 (option 1 on the diagram) or, if he is covered, taking a shot that gives X2 a chance to rebound (option 2). Note that O1, O2 and O3 are beginning the drill at the same time as the X's from the opposite side of the ice.

Raider Drill – Players push each other in two ways here. The puck carriers are pushed by the back-checkers and the offensive players are pushed into quick transition every time two new players start out. This is a great conditioning drill as well!

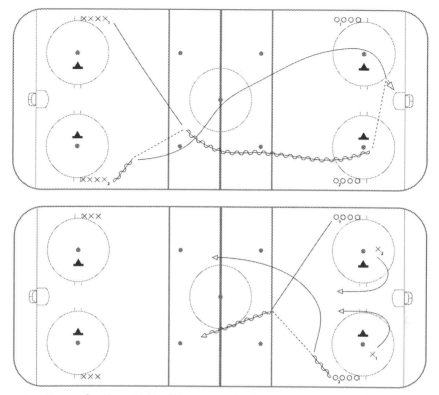

Instructions: On the whistle, X1 crosses the ice, receives a pass from X2 and carries the puck around the far pylon. X2 must skate hard for the pylon on the other side of the ice. X1 can make the cross ice pass or shoot. As the play is made, the coach blows the whistle signaling O1 and O2 to begin the sequence in the other direction. X1 and X2 must stop quickly, transition and backcheck hard up the middle of the ice.

Battling Drills

These are highly competitive and extremely important for attaining game conditioning. I like to include them once the players are warmed up and the tempo is high. They may also be appropriate at the end of a practice when you want to finish up with a little friendly competition.

Wild 1-on-1 – This is actually a combination of two different one on one drills. I set it up this way to minimize players getting checked into the player's benches and risking injuries. It also provides some variety for the players as they alternate sides and they won't tire out as quickly. The portion of the drill that requires the defender to close the gap and finish the check against the boards is done away from the benches where the glass is high (F1 and D1 on the illustration). The portion of the drill on the other side of the ice provides great gap control practice (F2 and D2).

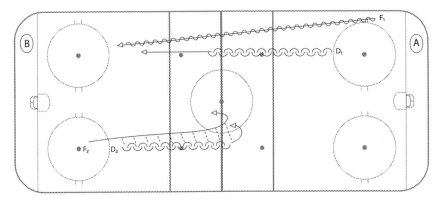

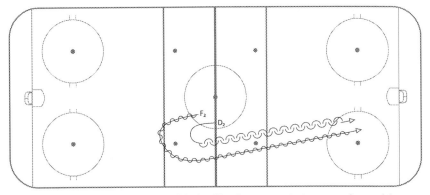

Instructions: "A" side: On the whistle, F1 who must start on one knee drives up the outside lane looking to beat D1 on the outside. D1 must go straight back to centre before attempting to angle and finish the check. F1 can't cut to the middle until the far blue line. "B" side: F2 and D2 make quick touch passes to the centre line when F2 takes the puck and turns inside back to the near blue line and then outside back in the original direction. D2 must keep good gap control and then play the one on one.

Olympic 1-on-1 – This is a very good drill for practicing agility and the quick lateral movement that is so important for defencemen. On the offensive side, players are encouraged to keep their speed up all the way up ice ... first when receiving the breakout pass and then while challenging the defender. As an aside, this is an excellent drill for evaluation purposes.

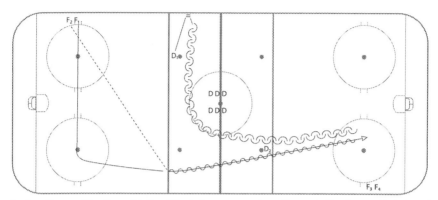

Instructions: On the whistle, F1 skates across ice, through the face-off dot and then up ice. F2 passes to F1. D1 must skate to touch the boards, then hurry across ice to achieve good position for the one on one against F1. At the same time, D2 will be challenging F3 who has received a pass from F4 from the other end of the ice.

Kootenay 1-on-1 – This is another drill that helps defencemen focus on good gap control ... and combines it with the need for quick lateral movement. Forwards must react quickly to the puck and once they have received it, they should be encouraged to keep their speed up. I remember former Edmonton Oiler Igor Ulanov helping us out with a practice one day and when I asked him what was the toughest move for him to defend against one on one, his reply was "Anything involving a lot of speed."

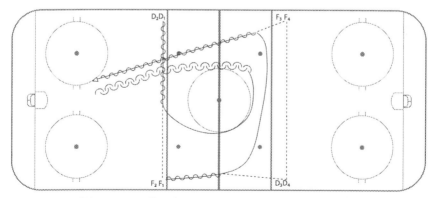

Instructions: D1 passes to F1 who passes to D4 and to F4. F1 follows the path of the puck and should get a pass from F4 setting up entry into the offensive zone. D1 must maintain good gap control and be ready to play the one on one against F1. At the same time D3 will initiate the same sequence with F3 who will pass to D2 and F2 before receiving a return pass.

Golden Bear 1-on-1 – Open ice 1-on-1's are important but during a game, defenders will see these defensive 1-on-1's far more often. This drill is great for practicing 1-on-1's from many different angles and to promote the idea of always returning to the front of the net … a good habit for defencemen to get into!

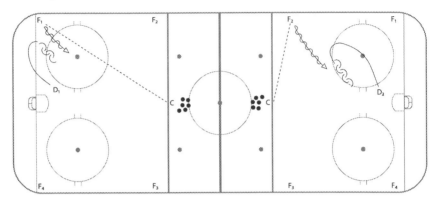

Instructions: D1 must play four consecutive 1-on-1's. The coach initiates each play with a pass. Initially, one is played from each corner area and one from each point area but the point of attack and the sequence of attack should be changed to provide variety.

Bull Ring – This is a very intense drill that the players will usually love. The puck carrier gets a chance to practice quick evasive moves and because there is nowhere to hide the defender has a chance to get tough and finish checks. Goaltenders must always be alert and they get great practice directing and controlling rebounds and handling the puck quickly.

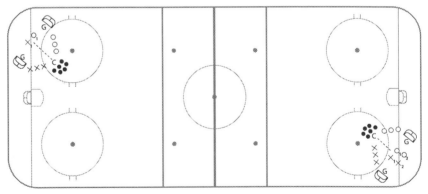

Instructions: The coach will spot a puck for X1 and O1 to battle for. If the puck squirts out of the playing area, another should be spotted quickly. Blow the whistle to change players at set intervals. Extra players can be added to make it a two on two.

Avalanche 2-on-1, 2-on-2, 3-on-1, 3-on-2 – This drill starts with some skill development requiring some quick give-and-go passes. It finishes with a straightforward 2-on-1. I use this drill to encourage forwards to experiment with different 2-on-1 options (net drive, "I" formation, cross and drop, cross and carry, etc.). Of course you will also coach defenders on how to neutralize these tactics!

This is also a very versatile drill as it can be easily adapted to make it a 2-on-2, a 3-on-1 or a 3-on-2.

2 on 1 Option

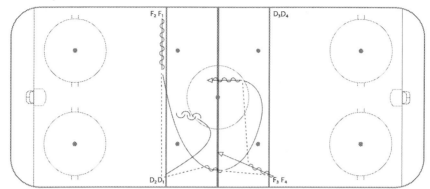

3 on 2 Option

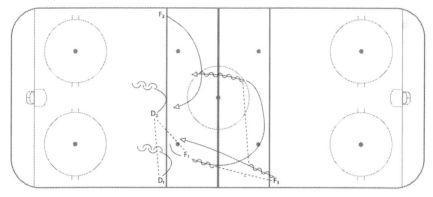

F1 crosses the ice and passes to D1. D1 returns the puck to F1 who quickly passes to F3. F1 then transitions and swings wide to the other side of the ice to attack D1 along with F3. F4 then begins the sequence in the other direction by crossing the ice and passing to D3. To make it a two on two, have D2 slide out into the middle for a pass from D1 before the return pass to F1. To make it a 3-on-2, activate F2 as a third forward to join F1 and F3 for the rush.

Red Wings 2-on-1 – I like this drill because the waiting forwards need to practice active observation and they are required to be in good defensive zone coverage position. It is also a very good transitional drill for defencemen who must quickly switch from defensive coverage in front of the net to finding a loose puck and initiating a breakout.

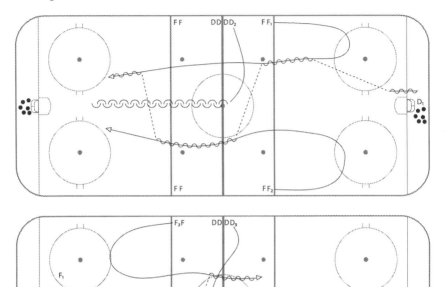

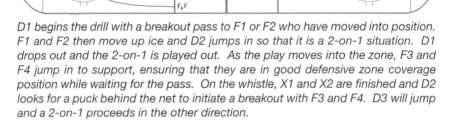

D1 begins the drill with a breakout pass to F1 or F2 who have moved into position. F1 and F2 then move up ice and D2 jumps in so that it is a 2-on-1 situation. D1 drops out and the 2-on-1 is played out. As the play moves into the zone, F3 and F4 jump in to support, ensuring that they are in good defensive zone coverage position while waiting for the pass. On the whistle, X1 and X2 are finished and D2 looks for a puck behind the net to initiate a breakout with F3 and F4. D3 will jump and a 2-on-1 proceeds in the other direction.

Pronger Drill – This drill emphasizes the importance of good defensive positioning when the opponents are in front of your net. Defencemen can work on tactics to front the puck (move in front of forwards in an attempt to knock down the puck before it gets to the net) and, on rebounds, move forwards from the area and tie up their sticks. Forwards can dart and spin as they fight for open areas and try to get their stick on the puck. This drill has changed significantly since the new rules emphasis which is designed to cut down on interference. Prior to that, the instruction to defencemen was to tie up the opponent as he or she attempted to go for the net ... but now that is being called an interference penalty so other tactics must be used!

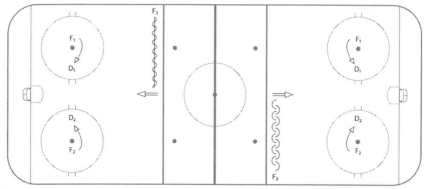

Instructions: F1 and F2 will go to the net. D1 and D2 will attempt good defensive positioning and be ready to front the puck. F3 will drag the puck to the centre of the ice for a shot. Any loose pucks are played out as a 3-on-2. Have F3 drag from each side before rotating personnel. Both ends of the ice can be used.

Fogolin 2-on-2 – My son Mark was fortunate enough to play on minor hockey teams coached by former Edmonton Oiler Captain Lee Fogolin for four years. I was also fortunate enough to learn a lot about coaching while watching his practices. This was one of Lee's favourite drills. It contributed to the effectiveness of the defence pairings on his teams. They were always very good at moving the puck and working together. This drill allowed them to practice staggering, regroup passing, breakout passing, gap control and finally staying in their lanes to defend against various offensive 2-on-2 tactics.

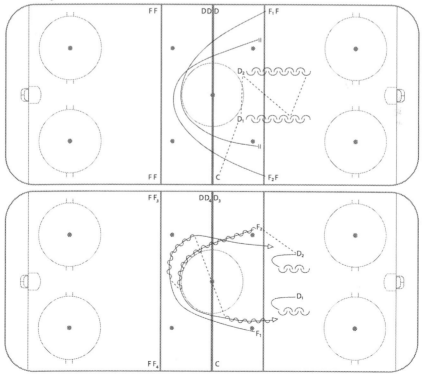

Instructions: The coach spots a puck in the neutral zone which D1 and D2 control and do some regroup passing back into their zone. F1 and F2 cross around the circle at centre and then set up to receive a breakout pass. Once they have the puck, they again cross around the circle at centre and this time make a cross and drop pass before attacking the defenders 2 on 2. The coach then spots a puck for D3 and D4 who start the sequence in the opposite direction with F3 and F4.

Dino Drill – This drill exposes players to a nice variety of game specific situations. It also emphasizes quick transition and is a great conditioning drill. It can be a lot of fun if you turn it into a competition where forwards have to try and score a certain number of goals in a set period of time and they compete against the defencemen and goaltenders who are trying to stop them. I usually have them try and score 10 goals in 10 minutes and the game is always pretty close!

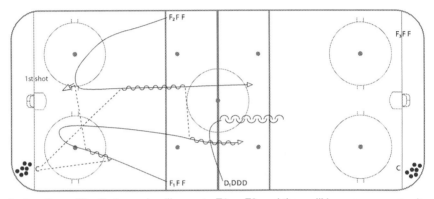

Instructions: The first coach will pass to F1 or F2 and they will have an opportunity to score on the goaltender. Only one pass is allowed so the player receiving the puck from the coach can either pass once or shoot. The coach then makes another pass as F1 and F2 transition and rush up ice in the other direction. D1 jumps in to make it a 2-on-1. The second coach will then pass to F3 who leads F1 and F2 rushing in the other direction against another defenceman (D2) who jumps into the play. D1 can backcheck in an attempt to make it a 3-on-2. A final transition sees the first coach passing to F3 who tries to score on a breakaway. D2 will be the backchecker in this case and will try to prevent a scoring chance. So, to recap, there is a 2-on-0, followed by a 2-on-1, followed by a 3-on-1 with a backchecker and finally a breakaway with a backchecker!

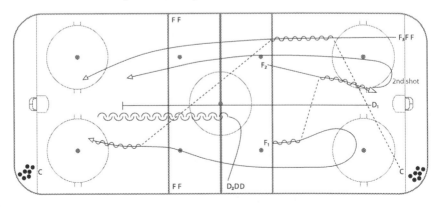

Dino Drill Continued

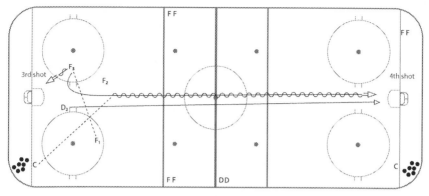

71

Systems Drills

For systems drills, my objective is to have players gain familiarity with the drill as quickly as possible so that they won't have to think much about its execution. Therefore, I like to keep this list fairly short. Why? Well there will be times during the season when you want to tweak your systems. Maybe things aren't working and you want to make a major change. Maybe you are coming up against an opponent and you feel like a minor change will be effective. Whatever the case, I believe that it is important for the players to be able to concentrate fully on the change without also having to learn the intricacies of a new drill.

Oiler Breakout – This is a great flow drill and it can be a good one to use as a lead-in to systems work. In addition to practicing a quick breakout, players are required to work on the neutral zone regroup and execute an effective dump-in ... attempting to keep it away from the goaltender. Goaltenders should be encouraged to communicate, play dumps and rims, and practice setting the puck effectively.

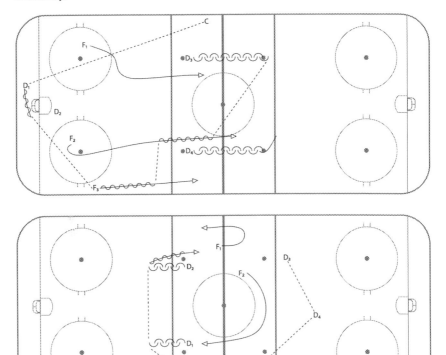

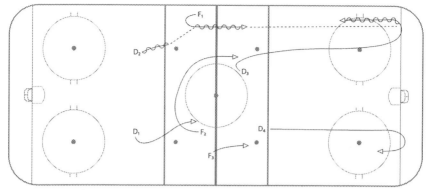

Instructions: The puck is dumped in for the first forward line (F1, F2, F3) and defence pairing (D1, D2). They all break out and at the far end pass to the second defence pairing (D3, D4). The pairing will regroup while the forwards transition and prepare to head back in the other direction. The forwards then receive a pass and regroup again ... this time with the original defence pairing. The original group of five now has the puck and as they reach the centre line, they dump the puck in and skate off the ice. A new group of five will skate on to the ice. The forwards will breakout with the second defence pairing (D3 and D4) and the new pairing will be in position for a regroup pass from the forwards once they have completed the breakout. So, to recap, the sequence is breakout, regroup, regroup, dump in and change lines.

Variation: Add a line of forecheckers to pressure on the second regroup. This will help the team practice the neutral zone forecheck. A scrimmage can then ensue until the original group of five is able to get the puck past centre and dump it in. The entire sequence can then begin in the other direction.

Quad Breakout – This drill is very important for me. It is a great way to hammer home the many different breakout options and hopefully over time it will promote creativity. Throwing the power play breakout in as the last breakout will give all players the opportunity to work with that and the 3-on-2 finish will keep the intensity up by making the drill competitive.

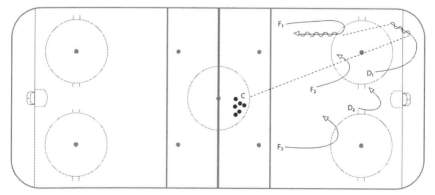

Instructions: The coach dumps the puck in and the players must execute a breakout. To ensure that the players are practicing all options I sometimes yell instructions as to the break out option to use ("Up", "Over", "Reverse" and "Wheel"

are the basic ones). I also will identify the forward who is to receive the pass from the defenceman ("1" is the strong side, "2" is the centre, "3" is the weak side). So for each puck I dump in I will yell something like "Over 2" which means that it is a D-to-D pass followed by a pass to the centreman or "Wheel 3" which means that the defenceman who picks up the puck will skate hard around the net and then pass to the weak side forward. There are three breakouts and the puck is returned to the coach each time. The fourth puck dumped in will be for the players to execute a power play breakout and upon reaching the far end of the neutral zone, the forwards will regroup and return to attack the defence pairing 3-on-2. As soon as they clear the neutral zone, a new group of five can be started from the other zone.

Progressions: Over time, I will add some forecheck pressure for each of the dump-ins. Also, I will stop calling the breakout ... suggesting that the defencemen communicate their choice and use the "Up" or "Over" when the puck is dumped deep in the corner and the "Reverse" or the "Wheel" when the puck is dumped close to the net.

Split 3-on-2 – I use this drill a lot. It is very versatile and it allows players to clearly observe team strategies. Phase one allows the forwards to practice different options for pressuring the net using triangulation. Either the centre or the outside winger will drive the net aggressively on the rush and players can see clearly how this tactic can open up the high man on the triangle. Phase two can be adapted to any forecheck strategy and while one side practices their forecheck positioning, the other side practices breakouts against the forecheck.

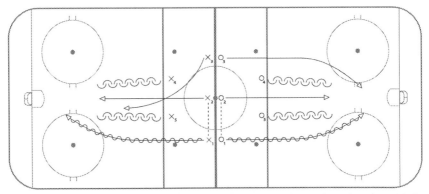

Instructions: Part one of the drill sees each centre with the puck and on the whistle, he passes to either winger who must then drive wide around the defenceman. The coach then will call either a centre drive (meaning that the centre must drive hard to the net) or an outside drive (meaning that the weak side winger must drive the net). The third forward will then cruise into the high slot and should be open for a pass from the puck carrier. There is a rush on each side of the ice and as it finishes, the coach blows the whistle to indicate that the play is over and players must return to the neutral zone. This initiates part two of the drill. As the players get to the neutral zone, the coach will dump the puck into one zone or the other. One group of five must break out and the other group of five provides forecheck pressure using the system identified by the coach. A scrimmage of about the same length as a shift will then ensue.

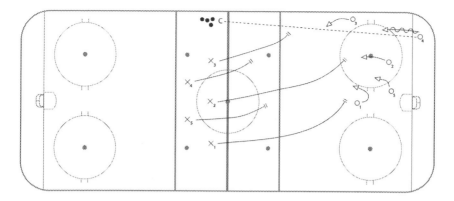

St. Louis Power play Drill – Players get lots of opportunity to fill different roles with this drill. They will all get a chance to break out and they will all work on their offensive zone strategies while on the power play. On the penalty killing side, they will get a chance to forecheck and they will all play the defensive zone. The drill can easily be adapted to practice 5-on-3 situations as well.

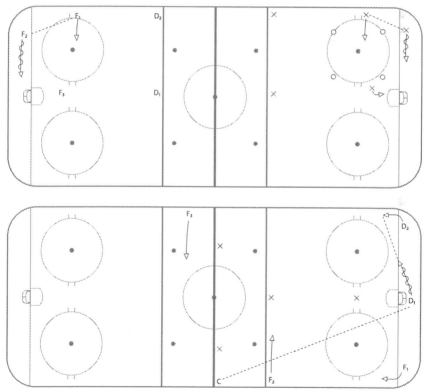

Instructions: At one end of the ice, two different units (X's and O's on the drawing) are engaged in a 5-on-4 scrimmage. At the other end of the ice there is a power play unit that is warming up … passing the puck around working on some options without any pressure (D's and F's on the drawing). On the whistle, the scrimmage is over and both units must leave the zone. A puck is spotted in that same zone

for the warm-up unit who will then skate down ice and execute the power play breakout. The unit that was on the power play for the scrimmage must then drop a player and they will be the penalty kill unit to defend against the new power play. Once the scrimmage moves into the attacking zone, a new unit of five players takes the other end of the ice where it moves the puck around using options and waiting for the next whistle.

Power play Scrimmage – To work more intensely on power play options in the offensive zone you can simply focus on setting up scrimmages from the blue line in. I like to walk through a few options before turning them loose on the scrimmage. I also like to set the play up from different starting points (i.e. from the half boards, from a face-off, dump in from outside the blue line, etc.). Of course the penalty killers will be practicing their defensive strategies. Working with two groups and setting up a head to head competition is often an effective way to keep the intensity high and add some fun to the drill. This can also be adapted to 5-on-3 situations.

Face-off Practice – Working on team face-off formations is important but unfortunately it involves a lot of standing around. A good time to schedule it may be after a good hard skate when players aren't chomping at the bit to get moving somewhere. Another possibility is to include it as part of dryland practice.

While watching the television coverage of the Oilers / Hurricanes Stanley Cup final, I was interested to watch a television feature explaining some of the practice strategies that were being employed. When the Oilers were having trouble winning faceoffs, for example, they had their centremen spend extra time at practice working on their quick hands in the face-off circle. A coach was dropping pucks and the player was taking one face-off after another. In the next game there was a dramatic improvement in the team's face-off percentage.

Both teams in that series were doing an amazing job of blocking shots. This is a very tough thing to practice because there is a high risk of player injury and you certainly don't want your team to be beaten up going into important games. So how do you get good at it? Well, some teams use sponge pucks so that the players can develop their technique while making it a bit easier on their bodies!

I relate these stories because I think that they illustrate some very important points about practice and team preparation. First of all, games are often won and lost because of the little things. If, for example, coaches neglect face-offs ... or shot blocking ...and the other team is working on those things, then that might be just enough of an advantage to make the difference. Secondly, you can figure out how to practice anything if you just use a little creativity! Having a big arsenal of drills at your disposal is a big advantage but you'll always have something extra that you want to practice so keep generating those ideas. Finally, I believe that it is important for coaches to continually be students of the game. There are lots of great new ideas out there and you can find them in a book, while watching other coaches in action or even watching a TV broadcast!

Chapter 4
The Game

"If you make every game a life and death proposition, you're going to have problems. For one thing you'll be dead a lot"

- Dean Smith, Basketball Coach

As a coach, I have found that it is important to remember that you can't control the game. You can have a huge impact on the intensity, enthusiasm and teamwork that your team displays, and you can prepare players so that they have the tools that they need ... but you can't control the game. There will always be the referee calls, the good and bad bounces and the uncertainty of the player's execution that will be intangible. It may be difficult, but the best thing that you can do is separate what you can influence from what you can't and manage your team accordingly.

Well prepared teams have a much better chance of success. We've talked about the importance of practice but preparation doesn't end there. It is important to have a game plan for each and every opponent. Let's talk about putting the plan together.

Pre-Game

Early in the season it is difficult to gather the information that is needed to plan thoroughly. You probably know very little about your opponent and there will still be lots to learn about the strengths and weaknesses of your own team. At this point, probably the best that you can do is discuss a few basic systems and then give players a few important reminders ... for example "go to the net", "finish your checks", "back check hard." Once you get further into the season, information is easier to come by. Here are some sources to consider:

- *Scouting reports* – if you have a scouting staff, this could provide you with a lot of information. Where you don't have a staff, you will have to rely on other sources (other coaches, parents). Either way, you should identify the key information that you are looking for and outline it on a form or checklist.

- *Statistics* – Over the last few seasons, I have had the opportunity to work with an outstanding statistician. His reports have been extremely valuable in helping me develop game plans. As a coaching staff, you should decide which statistics will be most valuable to you and then provide clear instructions to your statisticians so that they are collected effectively and consistently.

- *Game video* – This is valuable for two reasons. First of all, it allows a coach to review what happened on the ice ... maybe providing the opportunity to see some things that may have been missed during the game. Secondly, there are clips that can be identified and shown as a means of illustrating important teaching points for your individual players and/or your team.

- *Coach input* – it is always advisable and useful to gather input from your assistants! As a head coach it is sometimes easier to just make a quick decision without consultation, and sometimes that is the best approach, but after giving the selection of your assistants a lot of careful thought, it would be a shame to miss out on their feedback.

- *Player input* – your veterans and key players often have observations about opponents that are beyond what the coaches can see ... especially in considering weaknesses and tendencies of individual players. It is a good idea to periodically sit down for a chat with them and see what they have to say!

- *Notes from prior games* – Sit down for a few minutes shortly after every game and make a few notes. You'll find these very useful for setting your future game plans ... especially for games against the same team. Include information on strong and weak players, and any information that you can gather on their systems and tactical tendencies.

Identifying desirable sources of information is one thing but you also will need to set a strategy to gather and use it. Who will collect statistics? Who will compile the information? Who will video the game? Who will edit the videotape? When will you meet with scouts, coaches, and players? Again the need for good planning is evident.

Once the important information has been reviewed and the plan has been established, it needs to be communicated to the players. Some coaches like to have a team meeting on game day. The advantage of this is that the distractions involved with the pre-game dressing room preparations are kept to a minimum. You should have better focus by the players and there will be some time before the game for the plan to sink in. Professional teams and some junior teams have a light skate in the morning of a game and before or after that may be the ideal time to schedule a meeting. If an early meeting isn't possible, the plan is usually covered during the pre-game talk.

To ensure that players are ready when you want to talk to them, set some dressing room guidelines. When do they arrive? When are they dressed and ready? Your game plan coverage just prior to a game will probably not be as efficient as it would be if there is a team meeting early in the day so it may be helpful to think of ways that you can reinforce the message. One idea is to post a written copy of the plan in the dressing room so players can have a look at it as they arrive and while they are getting ready. Another good idea is to brief your captains and assistant captains before talking to the rest of the team. This sets up an informal means of communicating some of the important information in advance.

An ideal situation to reinforce your plan is to have it set early enough so that you can use practice time to help you prepare. If you do this, your game day discussions will just need to be reminders about what was discussed previously. And speaking of reminders, it usually isn't enough to put the information out there once. Teams generally need to hear about it on the bench and in the dressing room between periods as well. Use key words and phrases to continually spark the memories of your players.

A word of caution is in order at this point. People have a limited capacity as to the amount of information that they are able to absorb and process. I have often seen the players eyes glaze over when a coach goes on too long and tries to get too much information across. Consider which are the most important points and keep the message as brief and simple as possible. It is also a good idea to get your assistant coaches involved. Presentations are generally more interesting when the audience is hearing more than one speaker.

"You can't win a game in your morning skate or in your pre-game speech but you can sure lose a game in your morning skate or your pre-game speech"

- Dave King, Hockey Coach*

Another very effective means of emphasizing important components of the plan is to have one-on-one or small group discussions with players, especially those who are going to be playing a key role in the game strategy. This accomplishes two things. First of all, the focus of the players involved is likely to be better. Secondly, the motivation of the players is likely to be higher. They feel important because they have been selected for a special role and will want to work harder to ensure that they aren't letting the team down!

Every athlete prepares for games differently. It is important to encourage each athlete to study what preparation tactics lead to his or her best performance and then establish a consistent routine. For example, some athletes like to arrive long before the beginning of the game and before the rest of the team. Being at the arena gets them into the right mindset so they want to get an early start. Mark Messier was famous for this approach.

Once there, there should be a stretching routine and some activities that everyone participates in. Trainers are usually involved in this and they should be talking to the players about what works best and the activities that they would like to see incorporated. Sometimes there is a light run. Often you will see teams running the arena stairs. Soccer balls or volleyballs may be involved. The important objective is for everyone to be involved and have ample opportunity to warm up their bodies.

Equipment preparation is another important part of the pre-game routine and you should encourage your players to approach trainers and equipment managers as soon as possible about their individual needs. The same is true for any medical attention that is required. These busy team members have a limited time to get things done prior to games and so if you can minimize last minute surprises, it will make their lives much easier.

As the players are dressing, there should be an ever-increasing focus on the game. At first there may be a little random chit chat but as game time approaches the team needs to be concentrating on the task at hand. Loud music is one way of pumping up the energy of the team but you need to be careful with this. It is not an effective means of preparation for everyone and as a matter of fact it might cause some players to actually lose focus. The bottom line is that all athletes need to find their I.O.Z.F. (individual optimal zone of functioning) prior to getting on the ice. Some need quiet reflection while others need to be extremely active! Everyone is unique. If music is a distraction for any of your players it might be wise to suggest that everyone who wants it should bring their own MP3 players.

The on-ice warm-up is a final pre-game area that needs some discussion. There should definitely be a routine and players should be part of the planning of that routine to ensure that it is meeting their needs. In particular, I would suggest that you consult your goaltenders to ensure that they are getting the variety of shots required to help them prepare. You may want to improve or refine your warm-up at times during the season. I like to monitor the type of start to a game that the team is getting as a means of assessing the quality of the warm-up. If the team is consistently sluggish in the early stages of a game, it is a pretty clear indication that they need to be doing something better to prepare. A change in the activities and drills used may be necessary.

Coaches need to use the warm-up to do a bit of final scouting of the opponent. What line combinations and defence pairings are being used? Have they changed from previous games? How does the goaltender look? Are any weaknesses apparent? The answers to these questions might help you fine tune your game plan.

Heading into the dressing room for the pre-game discussion it is useful to have a game planning sheet that provides pertinent information about the teams and some important details of the game plan. A sample is provided as an illustration.

Coaches Game Sheet - Front

On the other side of the game sheet, it is helpful to have room for notes, drawings and statistics that are useful to track. This will be filled in as the game proceeds.

Coaches Game Sheet – Back

Plus/Minus	Period Notes	Team Play Strategies

1st Period	1st Period	
+ / - ___ ___ ___ ___ ___ PP / PK	_____	
+ / - ___ ___ ___ ___ ___ PP / PK	_____	
+ / - ___ ___ ___ ___ ___ PP / PK	_____	
+ / - ___ ___ ___ ___ ___ PP / PK	_____	
+ / - ___ ___ ___ ___ ___ PP / PK	_____	
+ / - ___ ___ ___ ___ ___ PP / PK	_____	
+ / - ___ ___ ___ ___ ___ PP / PK	_____	

2nd Period	2nd Period	
+ / - ___ ___ ___ ___ ___ PP / PK	_____	
+ / - ___ ___ ___ ___ ___ PP / PK	_____	
+ / - ___ ___ ___ ___ ___ PP / PK	_____	
+ / - ___ ___ ___ ___ ___ PP / PK	_____	
+ / - ___ ___ ___ ___ ___ PP / PK	_____	
+ / - ___ ___ ___ ___ ___ PP / PK	_____	
+ / - ___ ___ ___ ___ ___ PP / PK	_____	

3rd Period	3rd Period	Additional Notes
+ / - ___ ___ ___ ___ ___ PP / PK	_____	_____
+ / - ___ ___ ___ ___ ___ PP / PK	_____	_____
+ / - ___ ___ ___ ___ ___ PP / PK	_____	_____
+ / - ___ ___ ___ ___ ___ PP / PK	_____	_____
+ / - ___ ___ ___ ___ ___ PP / PK	_____	_____
+ / - ___ ___ ___ ___ ___ PP / PK	_____	_____
+ / - ___ ___ ___ ___ ___ PP / PK	_____	_____

After the warm-up, the last words in the dressing room should be concise and to the point. You have probably discussed the details previously so detail isn't necessary but having the key ingredients to the game plan fresh in everyone's mind is a good way to start the game. Just before heading out onto the ice there should be some time for quiet reflection. This can be an individual process or a team ritual. Some teams get together for a team prayer or meditation. Whatever the process, it is desirable to do something to open up the subconscious mind and let creativity flow so players can get themselves into the zone, the mindset that athletes are in when they are giving their peak performance. Most teams follow up with a chant or a cheer to reinforce solidarity and get the adrenaline flowing …and then it is game on!

During the Game

So the plan is in place and the game begins. Usually, as long as the game is going well a team will want to stick with the game plan. You never know when the situation will call for a change in plan, however, and effective coaches will know when and how to implement the change.

It is interesting to watch different coaches in action during the game. Some are extremely patient. They will stubbornly stick with their original plan long past the point where most observers would want to throw in the towel and make wholesale changes. Others start tinkering and experimenting with the plan sooner than observers believe that they should. The advantage to the conservative approach is that your players are familiar with the game plan. They have practiced it, they have talked about it and they should be able to execute it. If it is a good plan, then eventually it will work ... won't it?

"Most players seem to do a reasonable job in pre-game preparation. I find that players need more help in maintaining their focus and readiness during the game. When the coach juggles the lineup, the player has to park negatives, reload and refocus to be ready. When working a bench, I endeavor to make comments to players to ensure their readiness"

- George Kingston, Hockey Coach*

On the other hand, after you have given the original plan a chance to work, sometimes a team just needs a change to create some momentum. Sticking with something that doesn't seem to be working frustrates the players and they may have difficulty generating the intensity and enthusiasm that is required to get them out of a tough situation.

When some change is required, there are some different possibilities:

- *Adjust your system* – Most teams will have more than one option for each of their systems. For example, maybe you want to create energy by going to a more aggressive forecheck. Or maybe you want to slow down the other team by going to a more defensive forecheck. There might be something minor that you can change to achieve your desired results or it may be a drastic change.

- *Change your tactics* – You may see an opportunity for change by encouraging the use of certain tactics. For example, having your team use a stretch man more often will pull the opposition defenders out of your zone and create more room for your breakout. Another example would be dumping the puck in more (rather than carrying it in) to help establish your forecheck and create more pressure on their defense.

- *Change your line combinations* – It is a real art to be able to read how well each of your players is performing and make effective changes to line combinations that will help the team. Again there are some coaches who are more liable to do this than others. Scotty Bowman, who won Stanley Cups with three different NHL teams, is one who I particularly enjoyed watching. He had a great instinct about when it was necessary to juggle his personnel.

- *Change your goaltender* – Sometimes your goalie is having a bad game, sometimes the team is playing poorly and other times there is just a string of bad luck but whatever the reason, changing the goalie is a strategy that may be employed by a coach. It is important to recognize, however, when it is a good idea to take this action and you have to be careful to consider the effect that it will have on the goaltender's confidence. Some coaches will pull the starting goalie briefly and give him (or her) the opportunity to sit and settle down a bit before changing back. However you decide to handle it, communication is very important. Make sure your goaltender and your goaltender coach are involved in the discussion about why the move was made. Try to talk about it at the time of the change and then follow up after the game.

- *Change the momentum* – Of course any of the previous four strategies may have the desired effect of changing momentum but what I am talking about here is pushing the right buttons so that your players raise their level of intensity. Effective coaches will know just when they need to make that motivational speech, sit players on the bench for a few shifts, double shift hot players, or give everyone a good tongue lashing to achieve the desired effect. It often happens in the dressing room between periods but you'll see coaches who will use a strategic time out during the game to accomplish the same objective.

Sometimes your team gets into situations when, no matter what changes you decide to make, there is little chance of a change in the outcome. As coaches we have all had the experience of enduring the agonizing wait for the end of the game when your team is suffering a one-sided loss (or experiencing a one-sided win). Another difficult situation is the tournament or late season game that doesn't really mean anything.

As tough as these situations are for a competitive individual to handle, they can, with the right change in focus, provide you with some great developmental opportunities. Here are some ideas:

- Put players in different positions – This is the perfect time to experiment. Moving forwards to defence and vice-versa is a logical one. One that I particularly like is changing centres to wing (and vice-versa) or switching the sides that wingers play on. It is amazing how many players move through the hockey ranks with a limited comfort zone. They have trouble playing more than one position or are only comfortable on one side of the ice. This limits their opportunities as players and, of course, it limits the options for a coach. Sometimes when you make changes like this you find individuals who do a great job of adapting and really excel in the new position. The knowledge can be extremely valuable in the future if the team runs into injury problems or if the coach is just looking to shake up the line-up.
- Work on body language – When a team is behind, you really notice that heads are down and shoulders are slumping. The team's bench has no energy. Players and coaches lose focus on the game. Nobody looks ready. As tough as it is, if you can talk to players about correcting poor body language and replacing it with more aggressive body language you can often see a change

in the team's energy level. Once players are able to observe the change and see it as a positive, they will adopt the tactic more readily in future game situations.

- Pull your goaltender – A lot of hockey purists might disagree with me on this one but the way I look at it, the opportunity to practice playing with six attackers is very valuable for a team. There are so many tactics that can be introduced and refined for this unique situation and the better your team gets at them, the higher the probability that you will be successful when your goalie needs to be pulled in the future. Next time you are down 5-1 with four minutes to play, give it a try! Who knows, maybe you will get a couple of quick goals and make it interesting. And even if you do end up losing 7-1 instead of 5-1, does it really make a difference?
- Set short term goals – If your team is down and out after two periods, why not use it as an opportunity to practice goal setting? Maybe you can set a goal to win the third period. Maybe you can work on face-off or special team percentages. Set some fun incentives or create some friendly competition (between centres on face-offs for example). Once players get their minds off the scoreboard and shift their focus to something else they are often getting some very good practice and it is amazing what they are sometimes able to accomplish!

A favourite story of mine involves my son Sean's elite pee wee team that I coached on summer. We had a strong team and had done really well in exhibition games but when we got to our first big tournament, nothing seemed to be working for us. We lost our first three games and were heading into the final game with no chance of making the playoffs. To compound the problem, the team that we were up against was the Winnipeg Junior Jets. Led by Jonathan Toews, presently the captain of the Chicago Black Hawks, they were the class of the tournament. Their first three games weren't even close and a win against our team would ensure them a bye in the playoffs so they were motivated to win!

It would have been easy for us to roll over and play dead against this team but the assistant coaches and I used the opportunity to set the short term goal of beating them. The players all bought in and we got them involved in strategizing and designing the appropriate game plan. Anyway, to make a long story short, the idea worked like a charm and we ended up handily beating the team that then went on to win the tournament. The experience was one that everyone who was involved with our team still talks about today. Furthermore, we gained lots of confidence and momentum with the win and went on to a convincing victory in our next major tournament!

One area that I pay a lot of attention to when I am coaching is the player's bench. A well organized bench is an important way of establishing how your team will perform on the ice. At the top of my list of important considerations would be setting the right tone. The words that come to mind for me are "positive," "enthusiastic" and "confident." I personally think that it is very important for players to hear as much positive feedback and encouragement as possible. It just puts people in the right mindset to get things done. Add in lots of enthusiasm and you have a team that develops confidence in their ability to do anything. I have observed many other benches where the tone is quite different. You hear nothing but criticism and complaints. I'm not disputing the fact that players need to be accountable and understand what they need to improve upon but in my opinion, a negative tone on the bench will wear them down over time and it may affect their performance under pressure.

"Most of my bench comments are targeted on finding players doing things right. What gets rewarded, gets done. I am always looking to give feedback that closes the loop between a video session or practice and the use of an idea in the game. That's probably where I'm most positive, most focused, most enthusiastic in trying to find players doing things right"

- George Kingston, Hockey Coach*

The role of each participant on the bench is also very important to establish. Who makes decisions on line changes and who opens the door for the players? Who deals with equipment malfunctions? Who fills in for the trainer when he or she is busy? What about feedback ... who is involved and for what group of players? These things all need to be discussed before the game begins. Once the puck is dropped, things happen very fast and if responsibilities aren't clear you can run into a lot of trouble!

Feedback strategy is an important thing to discuss with your coaches. If one coach on the bench is yelling and screaming and another is trying to calmly get his or her point across, there may be some confusion or friction among the players. Don't get me wrong ... a little variety in approach is fine but as coaches you should discuss what seems to work best for individual players. One player may need a quick kick in the butt while another may not understand exactly what is expected and may need more of a detailed explanation.

An interesting approach that I observed one of my assistants using was kind of a shift commentary with players on the bench. While the game is going on, he pulls one or more players on the bench aside and has them observe another player on the ice. He makes comments and raises questions about that player as the shift goes on and the observers can learn from his or her mistakes (or great plays). I particularly like this approach because it promotes active observation ... a concept that was discussed previously as a very effective learning technique.

"During the perfect game I am standing and watching and knowing that the players are completely in sync with each other. I am basically rolling the lines. You know when that is happening and you should just let it flow. You feel that you're not coaching. It feels like the players are in control and you just expect it"

- Ken Hitchcock, Hockey Coach*

There will always be critical situations that arise during the course of a game. Therefore, it is of particular importance to consider how you will quickly and efficiently get the strategy required at these times across to your players on the bench. You are not likely to implement a totally new plan. Most possible changes will have been discussed previously and probably worked on in practices. But there are always instructions that you will need to get across in the heat of the battle and you won't have much time to do it! Therefore, good organization is of particular importance. Identify critical situations (i.e. start of the period, end of the period, last minute of the game, overtime, key faceoffs, etc.) and make sure that you have a basic plan for each of them. Then ensure that you identify the coach who will take control of the bench and get the message across to the players so that the plan is properly executed.

Another big factor to consider as part of your bench management strategy is how to deal with referees. I can't think of too many things that have the potential for getting a team off of its game more than referee calls but as a coach, you have a tremendous impact on how your team will react to them. Required viewing for anyone who has coaching aspirations should be the 2002 Olympic gold medal game of women's hockey. The Canadian coach Danielle Sauvageau did an absolutely remarkable job of keeping her cool through a long string of penalty calls that went against her team. As a result, her players stayed on track, stuck to the game plan and eventually prevailed to win the gold medal. It would have been so easy for her to get upset at the referees (and I have seen it happen with other coaches many times) and her players, observing that, could have lost focus on the task at hand.

Analysis of referee tendencies and developing an appropriate strategy for dealing with different styles is something that a coach definitely needs to consider. Some referees will call everything they see while others will let many infractions go. Some need to have total control of the game and refuse to hear any comments that coaches have while others will communicate readily. Knowing referee tendencies and making the appropriate adjustments to your approach to them (perhaps even making that part of your game strategy) may pay off in a tight situation. At the very least, you should establish who is responsible for communicating with the referee. For everybody else on the team, set rules and guidelines to ensure that the team doesn't get off of its game. Personally, I like to keep a very tight lid on this. If one person starts yapping at the referee, it isn't long before others join in and pretty soon the bench is out of control.

Speaking of yapping, it is another interesting study to observe players talking to opponents during the game. Some players are very vocal and the commentary seems to go on after every stoppage of play. Other players seem to just quietly go on about their business. In some cases, trash talking can have the desired effect of distracting another player, but it must be used with caution. It can also be a motivator for the other team. Furthermore, if your players get too caught up in it, there will be a detrimental effect on their focus. Unless it is part of your overall game strategy (i.e. some opponents may be easier to get off of their game than others), I would suggest that you live by the credo that you "never do or say anything to motivate the other team."

Effective use of dressing room time is another important consideration for a coach during the game. We talked about the pre-game talk and how the dressing room is used to get the game plan across ... but what about the time between periods? You have a relatively short time while the ice is being resurfaced and often there is a lot of ground that you would like to cover. It is important to set priorities.

When the players first get off the ice, they will need some time to deal with their equipment, get some water and blow off a little steam. I like to give them a few minutes to do that while I confer with my staff. First of all I will get input from my assistants. When I have spotters and/or statisticians in the stands I will want to have a word with them. When there is game video, there may be a few key segments that I will want to have a look at. Getting through all of this by itself could easily take the whole intermission so it is important to be efficient and focus on the most important things. Once you have gathered all of the information that you need, you will have to make a decision on the type of message that you want to get across.

So you are facing a time limitation and there is a limited capacity for player's to absorb a lot of information. How do you prioritize? Well, if the team is working hard but they are just being frustrated in their execution, it may be that you only need to make a few technical adjustments. This will usually be done on a white board for all to see. If it is just one or a few key players who need to make an adjustment, I find that it is good idea to just pull them aside to give instructions. By doing this it will ensure that they get the message clearly, and it will help to cut down on information overload for the rest of the team.

Video is a great tool and some teams are able to edit and display video very quickly. If that is the case, you may be able to illustrate your between period points even more effectively. Teams at the minor hockey level aren't likely to have the budget or expertise for this (although the new technology is getting less expensive and is consistently getting easier to use) but in recent years it is used widely by most professional and junior teams.

If intensity is the problem with your team, you will probably need to consider a different approach. This is where psychology comes into the picture! I have seen many coaches use their between period time for yelling and criticizing. This approach may motivate players in the short term. Nobody likes to be yelled at and so to avoid that, a player will often put in the extra effort that the coach is looking for. The trouble with this negative approach is that when it is overused, many players will lose their confidence if they feel that anything that they do isn't good enough. Other players will react to it by just tuning the coach out. They expect to be yelled at, and so their defensive mechanism is to just ignore it. Pretty soon the players on the team are just playing for themselves and anything that the coach has to say falls on deaf ears.

The positive approach is to identify what is being done well and praise the players for that. Once they have the feeling that things aren't as bad as they might have thought, it might be easier to inject some ideas for improvement. If the players leave with the idea that they are just a few minor adjustments away from the level of play that will make them successful, they will often have the right mindset to add the intensity that is needed. So what approach is the best one to use? Well, you will probably find most coaches on the continuum between "always negative" and "always positive." You need to find the balance that works best for you ... and your team. For many years, when I was coaching the younger players, I had a group that would respond to the "always positive" approach. I very rarely needed to raise my voice. As I moved into the older age groups I found that they more often were in need of a wake up call or an attitude adjustment. It depended on the team, however. There are a lot of factors that you need to look at each season, and at different times within a season. Some teams need more attention or a different approach, than others. The bottom line is that you need to find the right balance for your situation.

If you decide that you are going to read the riot act, and rant about all the things that are wrong, then make sure that the players also know how they can go about fixing the problem! I would suggest the "good cop, bad cop" approach. The bad cop scolds the players for playing poorly and then the good cop steps in to explain how to improve. You can often involve your assistant coaches in this. However you approach things, it is important to ensure that you are never attacking the character of a player. Calling someone a "terrible excuse for a hockey player" is much different from suggesting that they are "playing terribly today." In the first case, you've implied that there is nothing that they can do about the situation. In the second case you are suggesting that with a change in focus, there is an opportunity for redemption. There is a big difference!

"People are human. If you're going to
criticize them, compliment them first"

- Bum Phillips, Football Coach

Whatever approach is taken from game to game and from period to period within a game a successful coach will very likely have instilled the "can do" attitude in the majority of his or her players. When professional hockey players are interviewed after games, you often hear them downplay a win or look for positives in the case of a loss. I see this as the ideal mindset. If you get too over confident because you are winning, you run the risk of losing your intensity or getting sloppy in your play. If you get too down on yourself, then your confidence may suffer and you might end up putting too much pressure on yourself. Many coaches will reinforce this by continually telling their team that it is important not to get too high ... or too low!

As the game winds down, the pressure mounts and there are often critical (and stressful) decisions to be made. We discussed the need to consider your strategies in advance. You probably do this before the game begins. It may be something that you come up with between periods. In any case, it is easier to make a good decision in a tight situation if the groundwork is in place. A big part of the decision is identifying the right personnel. Usually a coach will identify his or her key players for certain situations and use them consistently game in and game out, but it is also important to consider which players are playing well on a particular night. Sometimes a key player is having a bad game and needs to be replaced by someone else. Other times, someone who isn't normally a key player is having a great night and you want to get him or her on the ice as much as possible.

Should you shorten the bench and use only your top players during critical times of a game? Well, this is always one of the toughest decisions that a coach has to make. Obviously, getting key players on the ice more often gives you a better chance of success but when you do this, you are sending the other players a message that they aren't good enough for the situation. This can lead to a loss in confidence of some players or dissention among others ... both bad for team chemistry! Another consideration is that over the course of the season, too much ice time can wear players down ... a situation that you want to avoid as you head into the playoffs! As is the case for many coaching decisions, finding the right balance is very important. Players understand that the team needs the right personnel to play in key situations, but if there are too many of these key situations or if the personnel that has been identified for them isn't doing the job then you may run into problems.

"We coaches have no bigger role than ensuring the confidence level of our players. The most important foundational principle of game play and life is initiative. For players to play with initiative they must exude confidence, courage and conviction"

- George Kingston, Hockey Coach*

Post Game

As difficult as it may be sometimes, especially after a loss, the team's first consideration after a game should be good sportsmanship. In a competitive environment, emotions often run high and it is sometimes tempting to blow off steam by yelling at the opponents and the referees in the case of a loss or gloat a bit in the case of a win. It is important, however, for a coach to set firm rules about what behaviours are desirable and acceptable. He or she should also act as a role model for the players. When I coached the younger age groups, I used to insist on everyone shaking hands with the opposition players and coaches as well as the referees after each game. In the older age groups, because players get so emotional, leagues often save the on-ice handshakes until the end of the season. Whatever the norm, it is important to leave the hard feelings on the ice and graciously acknowledge the efforts of the other participants in the game.

After leaving the ice, you will want to consider what should be part of your routine. Of course the players will need time to unwind. They will also want to have some water, and probably food, to replenish their energy levels. They should be aware of what type of food will most effectively replenish the body and when it should be eaten. A good nutritionist would be a valuable consultant to provide advice on this. Generally speaking, it is important to replenish the body with carbohydrates after a tough game and you should eat something substantial as soon as possible ... no longer than two hours after the end of the game.

Another consideration is lactic acid build-up in the muscles. It is the biggest culprit when players experience fatigue from one game to the next. Surprisingly, the best thing to avoid the build-up of excess lactic acid is to keep the muscles active and let them gradually cool down. To accomplish this, it is common to see players of elite teams put on some work out gear and go for a light ride on the stationary bike immediately after the game ... especially when they have another game the next day. Again an expert such as an exercise physiologist would be a valuable consultant for the team.

In the dressing room, coaches usually want to say a few words to sum up the game. You will have decisions to make here. Do you talk about the specifics of strategy or will you focus on the overall effort of the team? Will you take the positive approach or do you want to be tough and throw out a challenge to your players? Maybe you don't say much at all. This can be a good strategy, especially if the situation is emotionally charged. Whatever you decide to do, you should consider the message that you are trying to get across and ensure that it is getting through to the players.

I will conclude this segment with one final note of caution. All of your communication with players should be made with the big picture in mind. I would expect that most coaches would tell you that ideally, the team will be getting better over the course of the season and their enthusiasm will be building. If players are walking away from the rink with a bad feeling about the team, it will fester and drag everyone down. We've talked about the many approaches that a coach can use to try and provide the proper instruction and relay the right message to his players. It is important to ensure that it never has a negative effect on team chemistry.

"I always tell them after the game, "Let's remember how hard it was, let's remember how good we feel, and let's remember how tired we are""

- Brian Sutter, Hockey Coach*

Systems

To outline all possible systems and variations is definitely beyond the scope of this book. What I will discuss, however, is the idea of using a few "core systems" that are applicable to your team in most situations. Then, depending on the circumstances, you can make the creative changes that are necessary. For these adjustments there are various resources to consider. Entire books have been written about systems and there are lots of coaches out there who have used or developed interesting variations.

On my teams, I generally start with the following core systems. As the season progresses, we may make adjustments to these systems based on personnel (theirs and ours), our opponent's strategies or the game situation. I'll put the systems into two categories … those that are designed to create turnovers and those that are designed to attack the opposition.

Creating Turnovers

Forechecking

My preference is to use a 1-2-2 forecheck system that is easily adaptable. Why? Well, I would say that a 1-2-2 is a good middle-of-the road system (not too aggressive or too passive). It can be aggressive but it still leaves the team with a good defensive posture in case the forecheckers are caught deep in the offensive zone.

I like to have my lead checker (F1) pressure from the inside out. He or she is supported by the forwards who are a little higher in the zone … (F2) to take away the quick pass up the boards and (F3) to take away a quick pass to the wide side. On the "over" pass, (F3) will pressure, (F2) will sprint to the other side of the ice to take away the pass up the boards or cover for (D2) who will be aggressive and take away the pass up the boards on the wide side by pinching if he or she can get there first. (F1) will take the high slot position to take away the wide pass and (D1) will take the proper weak side positioning.

1-2-2 Forecheck

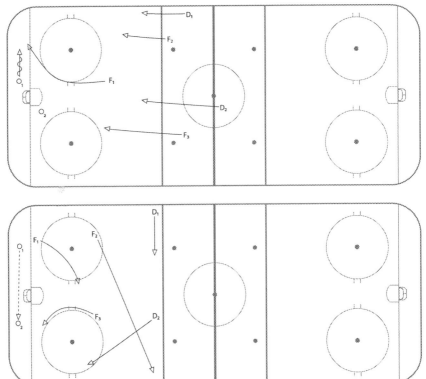

If I want to get more aggressive, I will modify the forecheck slightly so that it is a 2-1-2. In this case, the lead checker (F1) will change pressure from inside out to outside in. (F3) in this case will pressure hard to the other side of the net to perhaps finish the check on the puck carrier or take passing options away from him or her. (F2) takes a support position in the high slot. This will hopefully create a quicker turnover behind the net but if the defender is able to pass to either side, the defenceman on that side will pinch and (F2) will move in to cover. This forecheck may be used to change momentum, to get more offensive pressure when a goal is required, or maybe to take advantage of slow or weak defencemen on the other team.

2-1-2 Forecheck

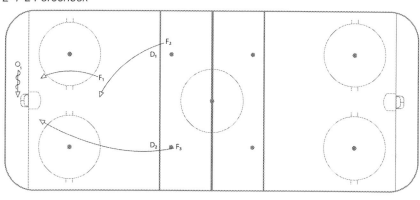

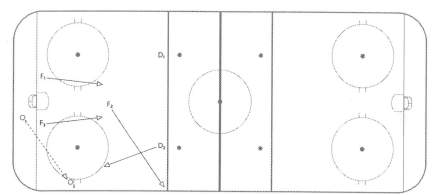

If I want to protect my lead, I may get more passive with the 1-2-2 forecheck. The first player in (F1) waits to angle the defenceman with the puck. If that player decides to pass instead, (F2) and (F3) are in position to move in and finish the check on the pass receiver. This variation is often known as the trap and it can be an effective way to slow down the momentum of another team, to protect a lead or as a frustrating tactic against an opponent who is very strong offensively.

Passive 1-2-2 (The Trap)

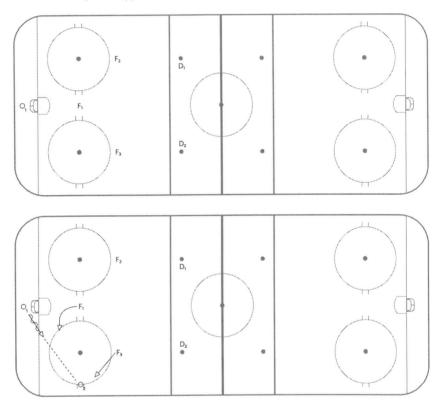

Forechecking in the neutral zone

The core system that I like to use when forechecking in the neutral zone is similar to the system that I use in the offensive zone ... a 1-2-2 forecheck. I find that it is easy for the players when there is consistency between the two. Also, I believe that in hockey, it is very important to slow down the opposition as they attempt to move through the neutral zone. Therefore, I prefer a defensive system which often creates more obstacles than an aggressive one.

The first forward (F1) is very aggressive as he or she takes an inside out route pressuring the puck. Proper stick positioning will make it difficult for the opponent to make the D to D pass. (F2) and (F3) will take away the outside pass by taking their position in the outside lane. The weak side defenceman can be aggressive and jump into the centre lane to take away any passing option through the middle of the ice.

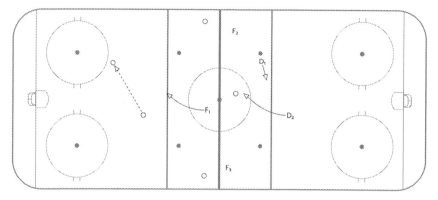

Defensive Zone Coverage

My core system for use in the defensive zone is a zone defence. This is a system that just about all players are used to and so they can play it instinctively and, of course, it is easy to teach.

If the puck is in the corner, (D1) will challenge the opposition and try to create a loose puck. (F1) is supporting on the defensive side of the puck looking to jump in and pick up the loose puck. (D2) is watching the front of the net and moving halfway towards any forward in the area who may in position to receive a pass out from the corner. (F2) is in position to take away a pass to the strong side point or challenge if the pass gets through. (F3) watches the high slot and moves to cover for (D2) if he or she moves to help out in the corner. In general, I like to emphasize pressure and so when they get the opportunity, I have my forwards move in aggressively (collapse around the puck). If the opposition has control around the perimeter, I have the players visualize the creation of a tight fortress around the slot area. That way, it is very difficult for pucks to get through and for opponents to gain control in this prime scoring area.

Again this basic system can be modified to meet the needs of a particular situation. One year, my team was having a difficult time because there were some teams with really strong point men who were getting lots of shots through to the goal. I decided to switch to a man to man coverage ... my two defencemen and low forward worked hard to turn the puck over and prevent passes to the point and my two high forwards stayed tight to the opponent's defencemen. As a result, we cut down scoring chances dramatically. Another year, I found that our small defence was getting beaten too often by big forwards driving out of the corner with the puck. The man to man obviously wasn't going to be successful but what did work was moving to a system with two low forwards. That way, any player trying to drive to the net out of the corner would be faced with two defenders. The high forward would usually be in position to take away the pass to the strong side point. This left our weak side point wide open but it was a difficult pass for the opponents to make and if they did get it through, we could usually get someone in position to challenge very quickly. Again it turned out to be a good change for the team and our defensive play improved.

Defensive Zone Coverage – Zone Defense

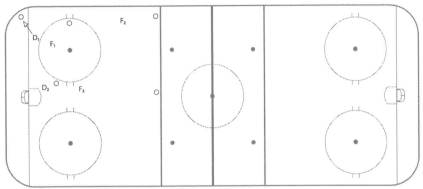

Penalty Killing

There are two components of the penalty kill to consider. The first is the penalty kill forecheck. A great forecheck can disrupt the opposition's puck movement up the ice and minimize the amount of time that they have to set up their attack in your zone. Ideally, your forechecker will get into their zone very quickly and create havoc in their end of the ice before the opponent has a chance to get the breakout started. If the opponent does have control, the objective is to deflect the rush to the outside and hopefully have an opportunity to pressure and create a turnover once the puck is moved up ice.

The general principle is to stagger your forecheckers so that one is in challenging the player who is initiating the rush while the other reacts to any breakout pass by forcing the pass receiver to the outside. I use two variations here, depending on the opponent. In the first, (F1) angles the player initiating the rush while (F2) takes a high position waiting to react to any pass that is made. The second variation sends (F1) to shadow the pass receiver who is swinging on one side of the ice. This should eliminate the option to initiate the breakout up that side and so (F2) is in position to pressure hard as the puck moves up the other side. In both cases, the defencemen are positioned to adapt to opponent's tendencies as they pass or carry the puck through the neutral zone although the defensemen in option two are probably a bit more aggressive.

Penalty Killing Forecheck – Option 1

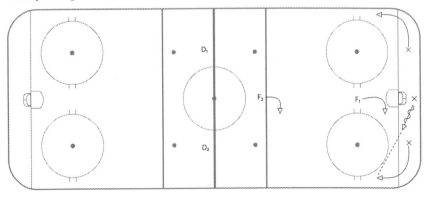

Penalty Killing Forecheck – Option 2

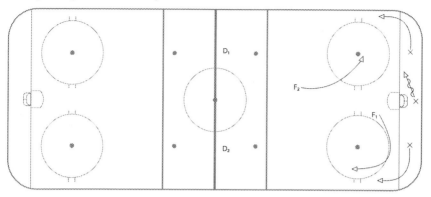

In the defensive zone, the traditional formation is the box which consists of two forwards high and the two defencemen low. A passive box allows the defenders to pass the puck around the perimeter and the players don't challenge the puck unless there is virtual certainty of retrieval or the opponent penetrates the box. The theory here is that the opposition will have a difficult time scoring if the puck remains on the outside. An aggressive box encourages players to always be pressuring the puck. As a player moves out of his or her position to challenge, a teammate must be ready to move in and support. This system can result in the defending team being vulnerable to teams who are able to move the puck quickly and effectively. The theory of this strategy is that you will be able to create turnovers and disrupt the opponent's attack more frequently than they will be able to exploit your weaknesses.

Penalty Kill – Defensive Zone Coverage (4 vs. 5)

When the opposition's defenceman drags the puck to the middle, the power play will often rotate into an umbrella formation. To defend against that, the penalty killing box should rotate into a diamond (illustrated with arrows on the diagram). The lead forechecker gets in the shooting lane to take away the shot from the point and the there is a defender on each side to respond to a pass to one side of the umbrella or the other. That leaves one defender in front of the net to respond to any pucks that are able to get through.

I like to use an aggressive box as a core system. I have found that only the best power plays are able to control the puck well enough to exploit the weakness of that system because of the constant checking pressure that is involved. Of course there are always slight adjustments to the box positioning that you can make based on the personnel and attack tendencies of opponents.

In a 3 vs. 5 penalty killing situation, a tight triangle is the usual formation for the defensive zone. Some coaches like the triangle to rotate, with the player who represents the point of the triangle challenging the puck at all times while others like to leave their two defenders off of either goalpost to prevent rebounds. In that case, the forward at the top of the triangle needs to move quickly back and forth attempting to get his or her body in the shooting lane. The stick should be active while trying to knock down the opponent's quick passes.

Penalty Kill – Defensive Zone Coverage (3 vs. 5)

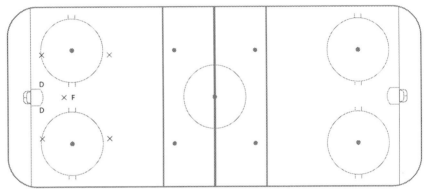

Attacking the Opposition

The Breakout

Unless you can create a turnover with your forecheck, your attack of the opposition will begin in your zone. An effective breakout will get the puck out of your zone quickly and set up the next phase of the attack which will be pressuring the opposition net.

One thing that I generally don't believe in when teaching the breakout is designating specific breakout routes. You can suggest options that might be open but there are many defensive formations that your players will be looking at over the course of a game. I think that the best way to be prepared for that is to provide alternatives that will allow them to adapt as easily as possible. Even when facing a team that has an extremely disciplined forecheck, there will always be opposition players in slightly different positions and your players will need to be creative in counteracting strengths and exploiting weaknesses.

My first instruction to the player (usually the defenceman) who is skating back to retrieve the puck and initiate the breakout is to go back with the speed and intensity that you would if you were going to rush from end to end. Of course, this will rarely be the case but if you are back to initiate quickly then it will be very difficult for the opposition to set up their defence. The initiating player is then looking at a few different options. He or she can start the breakout through a quick pass "up" the same side of the ice or by "wheeling" to the other side of the ice. Alternatively, the puck can be quickly passed to the defensive partner using an "over" pass or a "reverse." That player will then initiate the breakout.

Breakout – "Up" Options

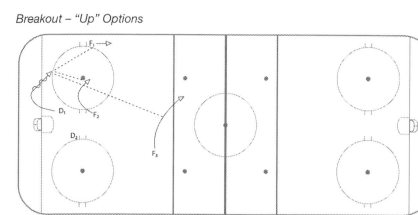

Breakout – "Over" Options

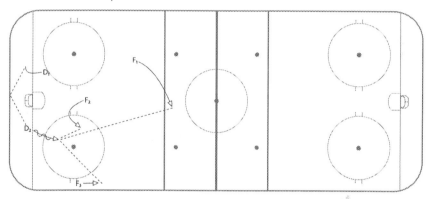

Breakout – "Reverse" Options

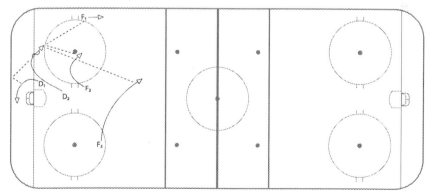

Breakout – "Wheel" Options

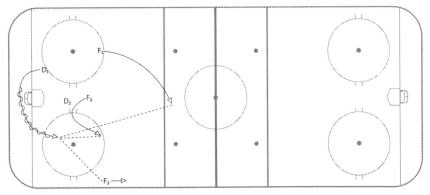

Once establishing puck control to initiate the breakout, there are basically three possible passes to advance the puck down the ice ... up the strong side, through the middle and up the wide side. Ideally the pass receiver will have some momentum and will be quickly supported by another player.

Against teams that use a fairly aggressive forecheck, these passing options will likely get the puck out of the zone. If the opponent is using a passive 1-2-2 forecheck or a trap, these options may not be open and alternative strategies are sometimes necessary. One way to beat the trap is for the forward receiving the pass to make a quick return pass back to the defence who then will look for alternative passing options. A second possibility is to use a controlled breakout. The defenceman stops behind the net and his / her teammates skate patterns to get into pass receiving positions that support the puck movement up the ice. In either case, the team breaking out needs to be patient and the progression is often slower and more methodical.

Adding a controlled breakout to your list of core systems is advisable. The one that I like to use is the same one that I use as a power play breakout. I will be illustrating that along with my discussion of power play options.

Offensive Zone

I'm not sure if it is best classified as a system but there are certainly strategies that teams will use to get control of the puck in the opposition zone. I tell my players that the most desirable option is to carry the puck into the zone with speed and control. A team that can generate speed through the neutral zone and maintain control of the puck is very difficult to defend against. Unfortunately, the opposition is usually seeking to prevent it at all costs. If there are defenders blocking entry into the offensive zone, the best alternative is often to dump the puck into the zone and attempt to regain control by getting to the loose puck more quickly or by separating the opponent from the puck with a body check. Rimming the puck or making a soft dump deep into the corner are strategies employed to get the puck into an area where the opposition is vulnerable and the likelihood of regaining control of the puck is highest. Whatever method is used, if teammates are aware of the strategy, chances of success are much higher ... so this should be discussed as a team and communicated on the ice.

Once control of the puck is achieved, the objective is to get to the net. Sometimes this requires some patience ... teammates can cycle the puck until a lane or passing option opens up. Other times a lane opens for passing or for the player to drive to the net. I always like to emphasize two basic offensive strategies for my players to consider. The first is that it is important for players who are supporting the puck carrier to go aggressively to the net. This pushes the defense back and creates a distraction for the goaltender. Often the player won't be open for a pass but he or she will certainly make it easier for the puck carrier to drive to the net or shoot and there are often great deflection and rebound opportunities. The second point of emphasis is to funnel the puck towards the net as much as possible. The term funnel was coined by Ken Hitchcock the year that the Dallas Stars won the Stanley Cup and the idea is that you get pucks towards the net as quickly as possible and from anywhere in the zone ... i.e. you aren't moving the puck around looking for the perfect opportunity. Many goals scored by funneling and going hard to the net aren't pretty ... sometimes unusual bounces and luck is involved ...but they still count!

Power Play

Most coaches could go on for a long time talking about power play strategy ... and it is an area that can change quite frequently over the course of the season as coaches look for the magic formula. Those who are devoting only a limited amount of time to practicing their power play should think twice about that strategy! Many games are decided on the effectiveness of this special team. My power play philosophy in the offensive zone is similar to my breakout philosophy. I like to give players as many options as possible so that they can be creative and are able to adapt to weaknesses in the opponent's defensive coverage.

It all begins with the breakout and to get a good start, identification of a good quarterback is critical. You want an offensively skilled defenceman who can initiate the play with an effective rush or a quick pass. He or she should be patient and let teammates get into support position. "Wait to initiate" is a phrase that I like to use. The formation that I have my players skate is a double swing which has the quarterbacking defenceman (D1) starting behind the net and stepping out with the puck while (F1) is swinging to his or her forehand and (D2) is swinging to the other side. A second forward (F2) is following (F1) up one side. As (F1) gets to the blue line, he or she cuts to the middle, thus filling all of the passing lanes and giving (D1) multiple passing options. Meanwhile, (F3) skates a stretch pattern forcing the opposition defence to stay high in the neutral zone and thus open up the ice for the breakout to proceed. If their defence doesn't stay close to this forward, he or she may be open for another long passing option.

Power Play Breakout

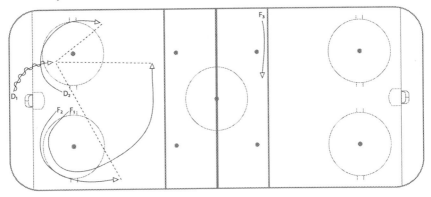

In the offensive zone, my core system is to have the power play set up on the hash marks along the boards. The player in control should be a creative puck handler who can see the ice very well. From this starting point, there are some low options and some high options that the players should be aware of. Depending on the tendencies of the penalty killers, you will hopefully be able to exploit their defence by using one of these strategies. Of course these, in turn, can be modified to adapt to different situations.

The low options that I set for my power play are as follows:

- (F1) passes to (F2) and then goes hard to the net. (F1) can then get a return pass or, if the defender stays close to check (F1), it will open up the ice for (F2) to carry the puck out of the corner and shoot or pass to another teammate. (F3) is looking for open ice in the slot or off the far post.
- (F1) passes to (F2) who moves aggressively behind the net and out the other side. (F3) can be positioned to create an effective screen on any defender who is moving in to challenge. (F2) will then be in position to shoot, pass to the point, or make a cross ice pass to (F1).

Power Play – Offensive Zone: Low Option #1

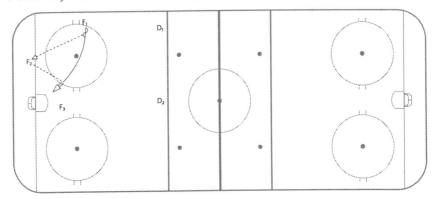

Power Play – Offensive Zone: Low Option #2

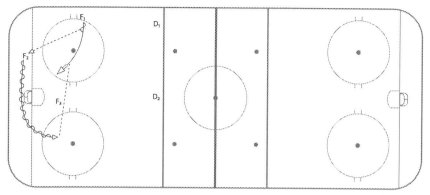

The high options that I set for my power play are as follows:

- (F1) passes to (D1) who drags to the middle. (D2) rotates away from the puck carrier and (F1) rotates up towards the puck carrier so that an "umbrella formation" is created. The other two forwards go to the net. (D1) can then either shoot or pass to the outside of the umbrella.
- (F1) passes to (D1) who quickly passes to (D2). This player has quickly moved over to the far side of the ice. (D2) then gets a quick shot on goal or can make a cross-ice pass to (F1). Again, the other two forwards will go to the net. Usually one will screen while the other may slide off the post for a low pass.

Power Play – Offensive Zone: High Option #1

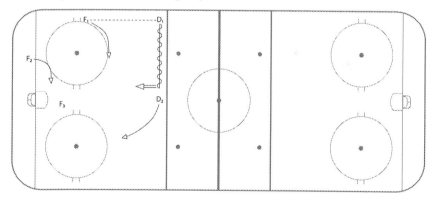

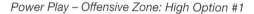

Power Play – Offensive Zone: High Option #2

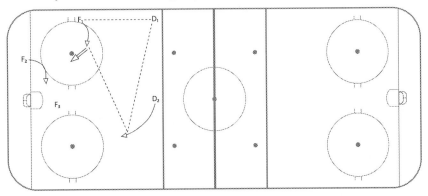

For a 5-on-3 power play, I like to set up a box with the two defenders up high in the zone and the two forwards are low and off the posts. The third forward is in the middle moving up and down the slot looking for open ice. The formation is often referred to as a box-plus-one. This power play is often most effective when players are on their off wings (i.e the left handed shooters on the right side and vice versa), thus giving them a better shooting angle. The objective is to pass the puck around the perimeter of the box and look to set up a cross-ice pass for a quick shot or to feed the player in the slot who is in prime scoring position.

In recent seasons, many teams have started to use this same formation on a 5-on-4 power play. Referred to as the spread, the usual progression is to pass the puck from the point (D1) down the side to the outside forward (F1). This player then has a number of options. Walk out for a shot, pass to (F3) in the high slot or across the ice to (F2). Either of the points could also be potentially open.

Power Play – 5-on-3 setup in the offensive zone (Box-plus-one)

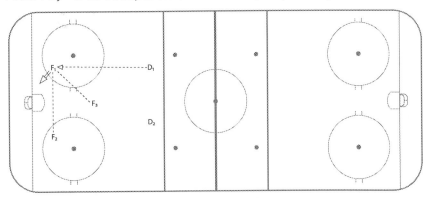

Chapter 5

Playoffs
... and beyond the season

"It's amazing what a team can accomplish
when nobody cares who get the credit"

- John Wooden, Basketball Coach
- U of A Golden Bear's Motto

As the season winds down, you want your team to be performing at its best. "Peaking at the right time" is a phrase that you often hear when describing athletic preparation and in the hockey arena, you want to be peaking during the playoffs. To get this, you are looking for maximum team cohesiveness and the killer instinct in your players. I'll define the killer instinct as the state of mind that absolutely will not accept losing as an alternative.

When a player who has the killer instinct is on the ice, he or she can shut out the outside world and just live in the moment. Those who have tried to describe it speak of how time seems to almost stand still and performance flows naturally as if following a script. The feeling can be almost spiritual. Paul Henderson who scored the electrifying winning goal in the last game of the famous Canada / Russia super series of 1972 speaks of it often. My good friend Rick Phipps describes it eloquently in his book Skiing Zen – Searching for the Spirituality of Sport.

If you have a team on which members have the killer instinct, you will be a formidable foe for any opponent. Obviously a coach would be looking for it. So how do you get it? Well, I believe that it all starts with motivation which ultimately develops into super-charged motivation. It isn't surprising, therefore, that coaches who are good motivators are the ones who are most successful.

So how do you motivate? Well researchers have outlined a number of possible theories. There are those who believe that individuals are motivated by need. At the most basic level, people are just focused on survival. Food, water and shelter are necessities and if it is difficult to get them, an individual will be motivated mainly to attain them. Once these are met, people develop higher level needs, for example personal achievements, and they become highly motivated to achieve them. You could use this theory to explain why an NHL team would acquire a seasoned veteran at the trade deadline in hopes of winning the Stanley Cup. The veteran's best years may be behind him but if he has never won the cup, then that higher level need may motivate him to levels of performance that he displayed in his prime. Another good example of how this theory works is in the goal setting process which was discussed in a previous chapter. If meaningful goals are set then the individual will be motivated to reach them because of his or her need for achievement and higher self esteem.

Another interesting theory is that individuals are motivated by expectancy. If they believe that their efforts will lead to good performance and if they believe that their good performance will lead to a reward that is valued, then they will be motivated to give a good effort. Coaches play such a crucial role in this equation. Players need to see that the coach is fair and will reward them with praise, more ice time or greater responsibility for that good performance or it isn't long before they are not motivated to work hard. At a team level, it is important that the coach selects the right personnel and puts the right strategy and systems are in place so that individuals can see that their efforts are leading to good performance. If the team has some success and the players can see that working hard and following the coach's strategy is leading to this, then it can be the building block for higher and higher motivation levels. If the team is not showing improvement, the motivation of players will die.

"I believe that success is always improving. You've got to continue to strive to improve"

- Marc Crawford, Hockey Coach*

"Your success is measured not particularly on whether you've won or lost, but on whether you are winning or losing in the process. If you see your team getting better rather than getting worse, then you're winning"

- Mike Keenan, Hockey Coach*

So having a good understanding of how motivation works will help us as coaches. It should be possible to motivate all players to a certain extent. We can guide them towards goals such as winning the league championship and that will appeal to their need for self esteem and their need for achievement. We can ensure that we teach good systems and celebrate when the team is successful in its execution. By doing this, we are illustrating a clear path to success and instilling the expectancy of being successful in each of our players.

But how do we get to the super-charged motivation that I referred to earlier as the killer instinct? It has been said that you can't teach the killer instinct. Some athletes have it and are able to raise their performance to a higher level in their quest to win. Other athletes just don't seem to have it and never achieve the greatness that is expected of them. Although some coaches seem to bring it out of athletes better than others, I don't think that anyone would claim to have the magic formula. In my opinion, however, there are things that you can do as a coach to create an environment that will foster the development of the killer instinct.

First of all, I believe that it is important for athletes to believe that it is OK to make a mistake. If we believe that mistakes are inevitable and that they provide us with a great opportunity to learn then they have less chance of dealing us a devastating blow while we are in the heat of competition. If you watch great athletic performances ... in the hockey arena, on the golf course, on the basketball court ... no matter what the venue, you will always see mistakes being made. The champions are inevitably the ones who deal with adversity most effectively.

"Adversity can be a healthy thing for you because it often exposes your current shortcomings. It can act as a wake-up call to things you have to improve on, either individually or as a team"

- Clare Drake, Hockey Coach*

If you are tearing a strip off of your athletes any time they make the slightest error, you may very well be robbing them of the opportunity to use the mistake as a springboard to achieve a higher level of performance. Instead they may be unwilling to take the chance that may put them on a path to greatness because they are afraid of screwing up. I'm not suggesting that you don't give them the kick in the butt that they sometimes need to sharpen up their focus. Furthermore, if they are making plays that are selfish or outside of the game plan and they make a mistake that can or does cost the team they should hear about it. However, I have often seen players make unfortunate execution errors when they are attempting to do the right thing. Sometimes they end up hurting the team but I really can't see the wisdom in criticizing a player for that.

The main question that a coach needs to ask when a mistake is made is whether a player is working hard and giving it the best shot possible. If so, then there should be praise for that and encouragement to use the mistake for motivation by suggesting that it will work out right next time. I loved the TV commercial that featured Michael Jordan talking about how many shots and plays he has missed in critical situations during his career. At the end of it he credited that adversity for making him the player that he became. If one of the greatest clutch basketball players of all time was given the opportunity to make mistakes, shouldn't we give our players the same consideration?

"I didn't fail, I just found 10,000 ways that didn't work"

- Thomas Edison, Inventor

"Courage is resistance to fear, mastery of fear ... not absence of fear

- Mark Twain, Author

I have continually mentioned goal setting and monitoring as an effective means of improving performance of the individual and of the team. I also believe that it is another practice that will have a positive impact on the development of the killer instinct. If athletes are always setting goals, monitoring their progress towards those goals and experiencing the satisfaction of achieving them they are, at the same time, developing the mindset that they will always strive for the best and refuse to settle for anything else.

I see creativity as another quality that is a prominent ingredient in the development of the killer instinct. It is unusual to see teams that don't have to make adjustments to deal with opposition strategies as they march towards a championship. Sometimes they run into some adversity but the ability to regroup and creatively find another path to the desired goal is so very important. Creativity in the team starts with creativity of individual athletes. You can look at any sport and see it prominently in top performers. Wayne Gretzky wasn't the best skater when he played. He didn't have the hardest shot. He certainly wasn't the most physical. Yet he was able to dominate the game because of his great creativity. Many people will say that it isn't possible to teach creativity. They believe that you either have it or you don't. Well I don't buy that. There are things that you can do as a coach to promote creativity in your athletes. Let's put together a list. Many are points that have been previously discussed:

- *Add creativity to your drills* – If you have a drill that involves skating and shooting why not add a fake shot? Or a tight turn? Vary your passing drills by requiring players to look one way and pass another. There are lots of possibilities and they all lead to ideas that will enhance a player's creativity.

- *Give them options* – If your systems are too rigid your players will become like robots ... always trying the same things. As soon as your opposition figures out your game plan you are in big trouble! Give them some alternatives and work with them at appropriate times throughout the season. This is the concept of curve ball training that was discussed in chapter 3. If there are options, especially ones that the athletes are comfortable executing, it is easier to adapt to the strategies of your opponent.

"For me, the game is too fast, too dynamic, too changing, too flexing and momentary for much use of system play. Players can use some structure as a start point to initiate offensive or defensive play, and also as a foundation to rebound from when tough times occur in a game"

- George Kingston, Hockey Coach

- *Use visualization* – We discussed visualization as a technique used in mental training. I believe that it is underutilized in hockey ... especially with young athletes. Most players get into the game because they visualize themselves doing great things on the ice. There aren't many hockey players who haven't imagined scoring the overtime winner and hoisting the championship trophy. Build on this imagery in practices, in the dressing room and on the bench and do it throughout the season. You can paint pictures that your athletes can use to create great performances.

- *Expose them to other sports* – There are a lot of skills and tactics that are part of other games and they may transfer favourably to the game of hockey. The more other activities that players are exposed to, the greater the chance for them to identify and use these skills creatively.

- *Expose them to other roles* – In practice for sure and in games if possible, it is helpful for all players to take on different roles. Not only will it give the players appreciation for the jobs that their teammates are doing, it may introduce them to skills and tactics that will make them more creative in their own roles. From a team point of view, it may give the coach some flexibility in setting the lineup. Many of the most talented players that I have coached during the years had, at some point, spent time playing another position.

- Use *"small area"* games – When time and space is limited, it forces players to explore creative solutions. I consistently run drills such as the cross ice three on three (illustrated on page 30) which force players to react much more quickly than when they are able to use the whole ice surface. Sometimes players have small areas set up in their back yards or basements where they can also work on their tactics. The most gifted puck handler that I have coached is Tyler Ennis, a recent first round NHL draft pick. His Dad set up a mini rink in the basement and from an early age, he was able to regularly practice honing his skills.

- *Set guidelines for off-ice activities* – This idea is tough to monitor as a coach but it is very important to work on! There are a lot of sedentary activities that, in my opinion, stifle the creativity of an individual. When I was coaching young players especially, I could almost always pick out the spaced-out players who have spent way too much time in front of a screen. Television, video games and internet should be kept to a minimum during the season ... especially close to ice times.

The last point is a good lead in to discussion of the role of parents in the development of an athlete. It is of importance that can not be understated ... especially for younger players. It can make or break your attempts to develop the killer instinct on your team. When you think about it, the amount of time that you, as a coach, will have to work with players is insignificant compared with the time that they are with parents so if they are not on the same page as you are, it will be an uphill battle. Have a parent meeting to explain your approach to dealing with an athlete and if you can get them to buy in, it will make your life so much easier!

I have made some of these points previously but they fit in well as points that you may want to emphasize to your parent group:

- *Be a cheerleader* – players love to hear about the things that they have done well. I believe that parents should never miss the opportunity for a pat on the back for a job well done. Even when performance is not as great as it could be there will be positives ... so focus on them!

- *Recognize the whole game* – one of the big mistakes that I see parents make is to focus on one area ... usually goal scoring ... as the only part of their performance that is worthy of praise. The players who will give the extra effort to make a check, block a shot, etc. are every bit as valuable to a team as the goal scorers but they often see very little recognition for it. Ironically, these less recognized skills are more likely to win them a spot on a team in the future. You can usually find players who are gifted offensively but it is sometimes more difficult to find the role players.

- *Make it fun* – I can't think of something that would be much less enjoyable than being confronted by a parent about the mistakes that I made after participating in what is supposed to be a game. Or scrutinized as if you are under a microscope every time you are on the ice ... game or practice. Yes, it is great to show your interest and support the participation of your children in a sport ... but give them some space! And remember that activities don't always need to be structured! Give them a chance to be kids.

- *Don't overload* – We talked about what a coach can do to prevent burnout but in many cases it is the parent who has the most influence on the schedule of a young athlete. Participation on a team is often supplemented by power skating, skills training, strength training, etc. and some parents take it all a step further by adding in attendance at a hockey specific school. Be careful!

- *Be careful when challenging your child* – If the coach is setting and monitoring goals, parent support can be very helpful! If, on the other hand, parents are involved in setting conflicting goals then their involvement will be a detriment. The most obvious example that comes to mind is the parent who sets some sort of reward for goal scoring when the team is promoting passing and teamwork. I suppose that there isn't anything wrong with parents assisting a child's development with subtle little challenges (i.e. maybe you could make as many passes as little Johnny) … as long as they don't conflict with team goals!

- *Build that "can-do" attitude* – Parents can be a huge support in this area. It is important to emphasize the proper approach for dealing with mistakes. And never let them believe that something can't be done. Athletes who achieve greatness are ones who dare to dream!

- *Monitor pre-game behaviour* – It is difficult to perform at your best if your body isn't well tuned. Setting guidelines re: diet, sleep and activities on the day of game will ensure that players are well prepared physically and mentally. If good performance follows effective preparation, the athlete will gain confidence and show consistent improvement. Conversely, if the athlete is not prepared and performs poorly, confidence and improvement will be compromised.

In terms of parents dealing with coaches, I think that it is important to establish some guidelines. Personally I don't want to get into an ongoing dialogue about how the team is being run but I think that it is good to have an open door policy. Receiving feedback is a great way to develop as a coach and so there should be a process in place that will allow parents to provide it. Regular parent meetings and evaluation forms are two ideas that I have used. Sometimes the negatives are difficult to hear but if they are presented constructively and you take time to consider them, they can be very helpful. And God bless the people who take the time to provide some thanks and positive feedback! Some of my colleagues have told me that they don't feel the need to hear that but I don't believe them. Everyone likes a pat on the back for their efforts.

I could literally write another book about the encounters that I have had with parents through the years. There are the unfortunate stories … parents who interfere so much that their kids suffer … either directly because coaches don't want them on the team because the parent is so disruptive, or indirectly because the kids themselves pick up on the parent complaints and begin to develop the attitude that they deserve some sort of special treatment. There are the sad stories … I once had the parent of a seven year old refuse to let him participate in a year-end party because he was unsuccessful during the last game in his attempt to reach 100 points for the season (a goal that his Dad had set for him). More times than I like to think of I'd see a player getting a scolding in the rink lobby, in the parking lot or in the car on the way home, because his or her level of play wasn't up to the parent's acceptable standard.

Of course there are the ridiculous stories. I had a parent threaten me twice in one year with lawsuits … mainly because he believed that our disciplinary measures for his difficult-to-handle fourteen year old son were going to have a negative impact on his chances of getting drafted and ultimately his future hockey career. Another incident that got to me was the parent who accused me of rigging the parent election of a participant for the all star game by suppressing ballots that had been cast for his son.

I would say that the biggest disappointment for me is to have parents, who have previously been friends, turn and walk away when they see me coming. I have had some who completely stop talking to me and hold a grudge for years. Despite the hundreds of hours that you spend planning your team and working with their kids, it is often all because of a single coaching decision that you have made. These incidents can make you wonder why, as a volunteer coach, you would want to put yourself through it all but thankfully they are relatively isolated.

And then there are the political stories. There are the parents who go to great lengths to stretch the rules, or even change them, so their kids can get ahead. Every organization has its stories, whether truthful or urban legend, about the parents who aren't afraid to use a little bribery to get a more favorable evaluation. And on a larger scale, there are some amazing examples of parents who quit jobs and uproot their families to move to another jurisdiction for the sole purpose of furthering the hockey career of little Johnny (or Janie).

Personally, I have an interesting story. As I previously have mentioned, I had a wonderful group of kids and parents throughout my youngest son's Novice, Atom and Peewee years. The chemistry on the team and their consistently strong performance on the ice made them the envy of other teams around the city. Unfortunately for us, the parents from these other teams developed a political strategy that they took to the Edmonton Minor Hockey Association. They were able to convince these administrators that it would be a good idea to force strong organizations such as ours to field two equal teams at the top tier of each age group rather than one. Their point was that more players needed to be exposed to the elite level of hockey.

The new rule was hastily discussed and then passed and enacted at an off-season meeting before there could be any real debate. Of course it had the desired effect of watering our team down. The end result was that it robbed our players of the opportunity to compete at the elite level in international tournaments during their final Peewee year … something that many players and their families had been working hard for and were looking forward to. It also caused a lot of turmoil in our organization which until then had been a model of harmony and great player development. Obviously I was personally disappointed by the decision but my point is that it is really unfortunate when meddling parents can have such an impact on a game that kids are playing for fun. An interesting update to the story was that a few years later, the decision was reversed after an influential group of parents decided that their sons deserved to compete at as high a level as possible.

On the other hand, if the parents buy in to your program and support the coaches it is extremely gratifying and you can see amazing results. I have such fond memories of that great group that I coached. The parents were all onside and supportive … and I have never seen a group of young players with a better killer instinct. Because they were so dominant on the ice, any team that came up against them was always playing at their best … because they had to be. I can think of so many times that we were "on the ropes" but time and time again, these young players overcame those tough situations because of their great will to win! Perhaps what is even more satisfying than the memories of them in their developmental years is watching the progression of the players over the last few years. At the time this book is being written, there are six playing in the Western Hockey League, two playing in the Alberta Junior Hockey League, five on full ride scholarships with NCAA Division 1 teams. Three have been drafted into the National Hockey League. Obviously they have retained that killer instinct!

So developing the killer instinct in your individual players is one thing … but the ultimate is to develop that same quality in your team. You quite often see teams that don't have the best talent on paper but they are seemingly unbeatable on the ice. They play together as a unit and have that intangible ability to get the job done no matter what the circumstances are. The term used to describe this type of team is "cohesive."

We will talk about a few characteristics of a cohesive team but at the top of the list I would put good leadership. Certainly coaches need to have that quality but it is at least as important to have good leadership from your players. Choosing the right captain and alternate captains is very important ... and it shouldn't stop there. Good coaches will also identify and work with other leaders on the team who may not be wearing a letter.

"Our captains had what you might call a propensity to be a leader or certain qualities that would let them move into a leadership role, such as their attitude, intelligence and their ability to recognize what is important."

- Clare Drake, Hockey Coach*

"A captain's leadership is demonstrated by the way he plays the game. He doesn't have to voice his opinion every day in the room, but if he competes hard in practice every day, follows the team rules, competes to a standard of excellence every night, and is willing to pay the price to win, you'll have identified your captain"

- Jacques Demers, Hockey Coach*

"I believe that leadership is believability. It's not trying to fool anybody. It's being the person you are, not the person other people think you should be"

- Andy Murray, Hockey Coach*

I believe that different situations call for different types of leaders. Someone who is a good leader in one situation may not be a good choice in another. So is there a list of characteristics that we can come up with to look for the leader of a hockey team that is trying to win a championship? Well, I would suggest that it might look something like this:

- They must trust the coaching staff and share their vision. They are the player representatives on the coaching staff. They need to support the coaches and work together to design the strategy needed to get the team where it wants to go.

- They must have charisma. They need to be trusted and respected by the other players. They will be someone that others want to follow. They play the game with enjoyment and enthusiasm.

- They must be inspirational. Often they are able to say the right things but even more importantly, they must be able to go out and demonstrate their passion with inspired play on the ice.

- They must treat teammates with respect. A leader will recognize every player, coach and staff member as an important component of the team and treat each one accordingly.

"Leadership is the art of getting someone to do something that you want done because they want to do it"

- Dwight D. Eisenhower, US President

If you look at any championship team, you always see an illustration of a great team effort but just as often, you can pick out one or more key leaders who were instrumental in getting the job done.

In the first round of the 2009 Stanley Cup playoffs, I saw an interview with Todd Marchant of the Anaheim Ducks. It was just prior to overtime in the deciding game of a series with the San Jose Sharks. The interviewer asked about stress and nerves in this tough situation and Marchant, with a big smile on his face, shrugged the question off. He talked about how well his team was playing and how much he was enjoying the experience. Not even ten minutes later, Todd's end to end rush and shot into the top corner of the net wrapped up the series for the Ducks. For me, that is a great example of leadership.

Another key component of a cohesive team is trust. Defined as "a positive expectation that another will not ... through words, actions, or decisions ... act opportunistically," trust has the following components: integrity, competence, consistency, loyalty and openness. A climate of trust is necessary for a team to develop the type of bond that leads to cohesiveness. This, of course, needs to be created at the top and work its way through the organization.

"Before people care how much you know, they want to know how much you care"

- Andy Murray, Hockey Coach*

Communication is another important piece of the puzzle ... and it leads to greater trust. We talked about the need for coaches and leaders to be good communicators but the lines of communication need to run both ways. Team members must feel comfortable communicating with each other and with the coaching staff. Coaches can foster the development of good communication by establishing an open door policy and encouraging players to use it. In the book Simply the Best every coach interviewed emphasized the importance of finding time for their players each and every day and they considered it to be an essential part of their coaching strategy.

Last but certainly not least, I would add work ethic to the list. When you look at championship teams in the National Hockey League, it is interesting to note how many of them needed to get to the finals and lose out before they discovered the work ethic that was needed to get them to the next level. In his book Champions, Kevin Lowe talks about how, in their first Stanley Cup final appearance, the Edmonton Oiler players walked past the dressing room of the victorious New York Islanders after the final game of the series and noted how beaten, bloody and exhausted they were. It was at that moment they realized what it would take for them to become champions and the next year they were able to use what they had learned to achieve that goal.

"In hockey, skill is very important and you want to have as much as you can ... don't ever downplay skill ... but hustle and effort can definitely, definitely level the playing field in our sport"

- Dave King, Hockey Coach*

An interesting observation about cohesive teams is that they have been through adversity together. The support of one another through troubled times creates a bond that strengthens and solidifies ... and the greater the adversity, the greater the bond. War veterans often talk about their special relationships to those with whom they have fought shoulder to shoulder, their lives on the line.

In the dressing room of championship teams you often hear talk about the adversity that the team had to work through to reach their goal. It may have been a prolonged losing streak, maybe it was an injury problem, or possibly it was an unfortunate incident that was reported in the media ... but working through that adversity contributed to the cohesiveness that allowed them to reach the highest level.

On the one hand, you would love to go through a season without a problem ... gliding effortlessly wire to wire. Realistically, however, it is never going to happen and a good coach will be able to reframe a loss, an injury, an incident and change the team focus so that the adversity turns it into something that creates a stronger team. During the good times, teams are generally loose and enjoying their time at the rink and life will be easier for a coach but it is important to ensure that you don't take it for granted. Things can turn very quickly. Regular team building is still important.

Team building is the term used to describe activities that are designed to promote team cohesiveness. Most often, they take the form of a social outing ... just getting together for a meal or a party and giving teammates a chance to socialize and get to know one another. Most coaches relish the opportunity to get out on road trips because, being away from home and all of the distractions of daily life, players have a better chance to develop a bond with one another, the coaches and the team staff. Trust building is another popular team building activity. An obstacle course that requires teammates to co-operate to get through would be one example. A competitive situation requiring teammates to work together to win would be another. Brainstorm with your staff and come up with ideas that you can work with early in the season ... and often throughout!

"We try to get the players to do three things: first of all, communicate with each other; secondly, find a goodness in each other; and thirdly, make people comfortable in uncomfortable situations. In the beginning they look vulnerable and are vulnerable, and then comfortable after they try these approaches because now the fear factor is not there. We try to help players take their guard down"

- Ken Hitchcock, Hockey Coach*

The cohesive team with the killer instinct is one to be feared in the playoffs. This is a special time of the season and one that players should have had in mind from training camp on. Let's put together a checklist of factors that a team should have in place at this point in time.

- *Physical readiness* – The program should have been designed so that players are at their peak in terms of strength, flexibility and cardio vascular training. Energy management is critical in the weeks leading up to the playoffs. If possible, it may be wise to rest key players so that they have maximum energy for the playoff run.

- *Mental readiness* – At this point in time the focus of the team should be clear. Setting goals, visualizing results and consistent reinforcement throughout the season should have everyone on the same path.

- *Finely tuned systems* - Every system should have been practiced, reviewed and tested in competition. There should be no confusion as to the responsibility of any player in any situation.

- *Contingency plans* – You never know when something unexpected will arise. For example, what will you do in the case of injury? Who will step in to the roles that have been vacated? It is always easier to adapt when you have considered these possibilities in advance.

- *Spare troops* – In addition to your roster, it is often possible to bring some extra players along for the ride. Whether they are to be utilized in games or they are just future prospects to be brought in for exposure to the team, they can add to the solidarity of the team and the environment of excitement that the playoffs bring.

- *Scouting of your opposition* – In most cases, you should have a pretty good book on your opposition at this point in the season. Where that hasn't been possible, you should gather as much information as possible to help you prepare.

- *Logistical considerations* – once you know your game schedule, it is important to consider how everything else will fit in. Consider travel, accommodation, and practice time and ensure that adequate rest, lots of water and good nutrition is built in to the plan.

- *Special plans* – Although your team has likely participated in many team building activities over the season, most coaches like to add something special to prepare the team for the playoffs. Here are some ideas:
  - *Team retreats* – Getting away for a day or two with just the guys allows you to have a little fun and solidify friendships but it also can provide a clear message that it is now time to change gears and take the intensity to a new level.
  - *Songs or slogans* – Having a simple song or slogan that will stick easily in the memory provides something for the team to rally around and is often a very powerful motivator. I can still remember watching Glenn Anderson of the Oilers belting out Tina Turner's "Simply the Best" in the dressing room after the team's 1990 Stanley Cup win. There are many great inspirational phrases out there that can be used. Here are a few examples that I have worked with:
    - "Whatever it takes"
    - "Dig deep"
    - "Refuse to lose"
    - "One shift at a time"

- *Videos* – If you have someone who has the knack of putting together an inspirational video it can be extremely powerful. My oldest son Mike played on a Junior team that went on an exceptional playoff run one year and a favourite memory of his is the inspirational video that the coach put together to prepare the team before each game. It was the last thing that the boys watched before leaving the dressing room each game and the players were so pumped up heading out onto the playing surface that their skates barely touched the ice! A few seasons ago, Mike was coaching a Junior A team. Prior to the playoffs, he put together a similar video that helped to inspire his team to the league finals!

- *Hair dye, beards, clothing* … these visible artifacts of the playoff run can provide continual reminders to players about the task at hand. I remember hearing the Team Canada coaches of 2002 talk about the T shirts that the players were given prior to the Olympics. The team rule was that everyone had to wear their shirt at some point during game days as a sign of solidarity. Some wore it at breakfast, others wore it for warm-ups … it was up to each player. What happened was that every time the team got together, the players were reminded about the goal that they all had committed to.

- *Other ideas* – There are lots of good ideas that fellow coaches can provide. My favourite memory involves a novice team that my son Mark played on. It had been a long season and going into our big year end tournament, I was looking for something that would give the team a boost. I decided that I would entice the team with the promise that they could shave my head if we won. Before every game, I would bring out the clippers to remind them and the enthusiasm that the idea generated was easy to see in the team's play. To make a long story short, we played our best hockey of the season and cruised to an easy tournament win. As an aside, I enjoyed the new "hair" style so much that now, sixteen years later, I am still sporting a shiny dome!

Playoffs can also be the time of year when it may be a lucky bounce that separates the champions from the also-rans. You can't control the bounces but if you, as a coach, can put your team in the position where you might have a better chance of getting that lucky bounce then maybe, just maybe, the hockey gods will smile on you a little more often than the other guy. Bringing in a set play or a creative tactic to catch an opponent off guard may just give you that edge that you need.

In the 2008 Stanley Cup playoffs, the Detroit Red Wings gave everyone a good demonstration of how important puck control is to success in today's game of hockey. Referees are calling more interference penalties than ever before and as a result, the skilled players have more room and are able to spend much more time with the puck. This, of course, results in more scoring chances. In turn, it will also put the opposition back on their heels and give them fewer chances. Logically, then, the team with the best puck control will have a higher probability of finishing on top.

The first chance that you have to gain puck control is from a face-off. Monitoring face-off winning percentages and setting individual and team goals throughout the season can pay big dividends when you get into the playoffs. It all starts with a plan. The centre must decide exactly what he or she wants to do before entering the face-off circle. The plan then needs to be communicated by the centre so that everyone else on the ice knows what is supposed to happen. Each player has responsibilities if the face-off is won and other responsibilities if it is lost. It is a mistake for everyone on the ice other than the centre to take a mental vacation when the puck is dropped. Winning and losing draws (face-offs) is a team effort and that should be emphasized by the coach.

Obviously quick hands are a great asset for anyone who wants to win in the face-off circle but body positioning is also very important. The rules of hockey dictate how you must set up prior to the drop of the puck but there are ways to set the body so you can achieve maximum strength and leverage. Reading the opposition's centre is also very important. Sometimes winning a draw isn't about quick hands and the best strategy is to tie up the opponent and use your skates to kick the puck to a teammate. I could easily go on and talk about many different face-off scenarios but the truth is that everything may change depending on the opponent's strategy and personnel. The important point that I want to get across is that planning in this area can make a big difference. I have seen many minor hockey teams that don't pay much attention to it and they consistently end up having to chase their opponent to get control of the puck. Having a coach who is in charge of the centres and can monitor face-offs from game to game is a very good idea.

There are many face-off strategies that you can consider but as was the case with our discussion of systems, I would suggest that you start with a few core formations and adapt them as necessary. I will provide you with possibilities for each zone. Face-offs with the goaltender pulled at the end of a game are particularly important and I have provided you with a formation that I use. For those last minute draws, an additional consideration is the personnel who will line up in each spot. Ideally, you want your best centre to take the draw and to position your best passer, your best shooter, the best net crashers, etc. where they will be of most benefit for a successful execution of the plan.

Defensive Zone Face-Offs

The most important consideration here is to keep the puck away from the offensive team so they are unable to create a scoring chance. Therefore, most formations will focus on winning the draw towards the boards or into the corner and away from the opponent's point men and the middle of the ice. I like to have my centre draw the puck towards the corner where the defenceman (D1) will attempt to carry the puck around the net. Here he or she can look for breakout passing options (probably F3 or F1 in this diagram). Ideally, D1 will pick up the puck on the forehand which will make the breakout pass easier to make. A variation of the face-off will have D1 pick up the puck and rim it hard around the boards. F1 must get to the boards quickly in an attempt to chip it pass the opposition's defenceman and into the neutral zone. There F3 or F2 will be able to chase down the loose puck.

Defensive Zone Face-Off Formation

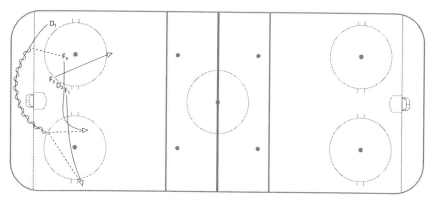

If the face-off is lost, the response of your team is even more critical. In particular, the forwards (F1 and F2) must get out to the point to take away potential shots from the opposition's defencemen. The centre must stay on the defensive side of his counterpart and both defencemen must quickly move to get defensive positioning on opposition forwards who are going to the front of the net.

An interesting face-off play that may give your team a bit of an advantage at some point during the game is the bench play. To use it, you have to have your player's bench on the same side as the defensive zone face-off. Then, from a standard formation, you will have your inside forward (F2) skate out to cover the defenceman but then continue right to the player's bench. Then you have another player (F4) waiting at the far end of the bench and he or she can jump on to the ice well behind the defencemen on the other team. If your center can win the draw and your defenceman (D1) can set up in a good passing position then you may be able to create a breakaway for that player.

Defensive Zone Face-Off Formation – Bench Play

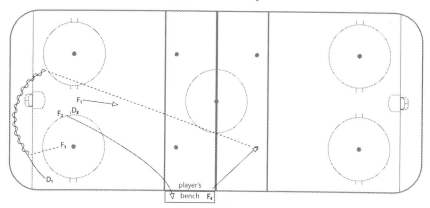

Neutral Zone Face-Offs

In the neutral zone, the team's objective should be to get control of the puck and get it moving towards the opponent's zone as quickly as possible. Therefore, I like to line up my weak side forward (F1 in this diagram) in the position of the weak side defenseman and have that defenseman (D1 in this diagram) line up in the forward's position. Off of the draw, the objective is to have F1 flare out to the boards for a quick pass from D2.

Neutral Zone Face-Off Formation

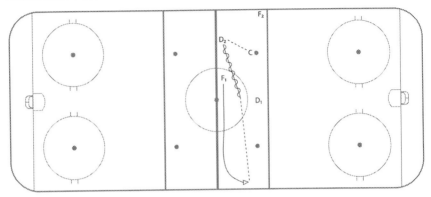

On a lost face-off, D1 must be ready to move quickly and cover any wide passes that the opponent may make. F1 is already in a good defensive support position.

At centre ice, it may be possible to execute a fast break play even more quickly. When the centre is good at firing the puck forward directly off of the face-off, you can bypass your defenceman and get the puck to the flaring winger even more quickly.

Offensive Zone Face-Offs

The main objective here is to get a quick shot on net and there are many formations that will position the shooter in an optimal spot to get the shot away as soon as the puck hits his or her stick. Many times they depend exactly where the centre is most proficient winning the draw to and where your shooter is most effective shooting from. I have provided a couple of other possibilities here.

In the first formation, the objective is to get the puck to the strong side defenseman (D1) who will drive the puck down the boards for a cross ice pass or shot on net. The wingers will support the centre to retrieve any loose pucks on their way to the front of the net. D2 will be available as a passing option in the high slot. The centre, after taking the draw, will drop back and support D1 defensively.

Offensive Zone Face-Off Formation – Option 1

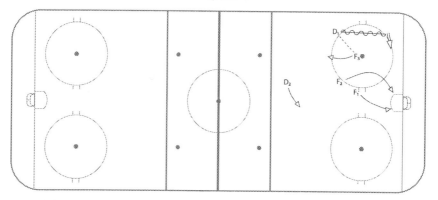

The second formation is very aggressive. Ideally, D2 will receive the puck and get a shot on goal but even if the face-off is lost, with four players up there is higher probability of tracking down any loose puck and getting it to the net quickly. If the opposition gains control, D1 must quickly return to a good defensive position and forwards must be ready to transition into a backchecking role.

Offensive Zone Face-Off Formation – Option 2

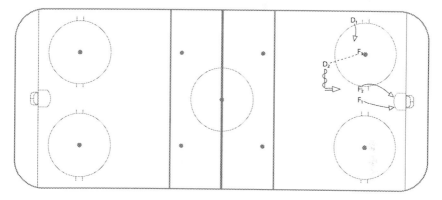

Last minute face-off

At the end of the game when your team is behind, it is a common strategy to pull the goaltender for an extra attacker. Puck control is obviously critical when developing a face-off strategy in this situation. In this formation, the face-off will go to D1 who can drag and shoot the puck, pass across to D2 for a one-time shot or, if there is too much traffic to get the shot through, rim the puck around the outside boards. The wingers on the outside of the circle (F1 and F2) must be aggressive on loose pucks and support D1. They then will go to the front of the net. F3 should get to the far post in case there is a rim or to get a one-time shot on a back-door pass. Ideally, the one time shooters should be on their forehand when setting up for the pass.

Offensive Zone Face-Off Strategy with an extra attacker

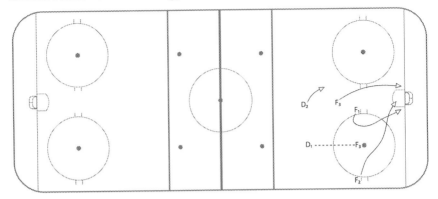

Another way that you can provide your team with that extra edge and a higher probability of puck control is to focus on matching your players against those of your opponent. If there are opposition players who are consistently creating scoring chances then it would be wise to have your top defensive players on the ice against them as much as possible. Maybe it is a line that you try to get out there ... or a defensive pairing. Sometimes a one on one match-up against a key player is the best strategy. On the other side of the coin, you may be able to pick up on weaknesses in your opponent's lineup. If you can get your top offensive players out against weaker lines or defensive pairings then you will very likely have more scoring chances. Matching is, of course, just another thing for a coach to keep in mind and if a team decides to adopt this strategy it can be very intense and will require a lot of attention during playoff games. This gives us another good illustration of why good planning and effective delegation of responsibilities is critical on an effective coaching staff.

Once the preparation is place, it all comes down to execution. As a coach, you can adjust strategy for each game and rely on your resources to make the best decisions possible during the game ... but as we've noted before, you can't control the outcome. Great coaches are the ones who can identify the best personnel and the best strategy to put the team in the best possible position to succeed. Really successful coaches often have an intuition, a feel for the game that has been developed through many years of observation. They make great decisions and chances are that they will win their fair share of big games ... but they won't win them all. If you can walk away from the season believing that you did everything you possibly could to improve your team and that they were as prepared as they could be for important games, then win or lose you should look at your season as a success.

"Success is peace of mind which is a direct result of self satisfaction in knowing you made the effort to do the best of which you are capable"

- John Wooden, Basketball Coach

Many teams aren't finished when the playoffs are over. Some like to extend the season with a tournament or two. I think that there are two categories of tournaments. The first would be the prestigious, high caliber tournament that is often viewed as being as important as the playoffs. The approach to this type of tournament would be similar to the playoffs. It probably would be considered as part of the seasonal plan and the physical and mental preparation required for the team to be at its best would be of great importance.

Short term intense competitions like this require special planning and preparation because everything is so condensed. A detailed itinerary including travel, accommodation, meals, rest, meeting time and practice time is crucial. Fatigue is a big factor at tournaments and so everything that you can do to minimize the effects of that and keep your team as mentally and physically fresh as possible will give you a big advantage. A good manager is a must to keep things running smoothly and deal with the inevitable situations ... I've heard them called "thunderbolts" ... that will arise and test your patience.

This type of tournament is very helpful for the elite athlete. It is a unique experience that can be quite overwhelming the first time through. With repeated opportunities to participate, however, strategies can be developed and routines can be established that will enhance the athlete's preparation in the future. Internationally focused programs like the national Olympic team view these tournaments as essential for athlete development.

A second category of tournament would be the recreational tournament. This is always a nice way to finish off the season. You are still hoping to perform at your best, of course, but preparation is more relaxed. Coaches are probably giving players who may have had their ice time shortchanged during the playoffs more of an opportunity to play a prominent role. Ideally, everyone involved with the team will walk away from this experience with a smile on their faces and if you happen to win ... well that is just icing on the cake!

Once you are off the ice for the last time, there are a few little things to consider as you wrap up the season. I think that it is important to sit down for a chat with each and every player on the team. Ask each of them what they liked and did not like about the season and take some notes. There may be some very good suggestions that you can use to improve your program in the future. It is also a good time to thank them for their contribution. Give them a pat on the back for what they have done well and provide some concrete suggestions about what they should work on in the off season if they want to improve as hockey players. There are often a variety of future opportunities that are available to players and it is very helpful for them to know which they would be most suited for and how they can take advantage of them. As a coach you will be an important counsel and mentor and you may have contacts and information that you are able to share. In the competitive world of sport, every little bit of support that you can give your players is valuable.

Your support staff should also be acknowledged. A thank you is always appreciated but you should also take advantage of this time to debrief the season. Talk about what you did well and what needs improvement. It may take a while but if you do it while the season is fresh in everyone's mind, the feedback is more useful and your planning for the following season will be much more effective.

Chances are that before you are finally able to put your season to rest, you will have a final team get together with some year end awards. Maybe it is just me but as the coach of a team sport, this is an extremely uncomfortable time for me. I would rank it right up alongside the mid season all-star game as something that I would love to do away with. Yes, it is wonderful for the people who receive the awards and I understand that, along with the all-star game it generates interest and provides recognition for the team and the league ... but I just can't get my mind around the idea of singling out these individuals for their performance after a season of preaching that hockey is a team game and every member is equally important to success!

In any case, identifying award recipients is a task that most coaches will be faced with. Sometimes the choice is clear. There is an individual who stands out so clearly that everyone would be outraged if he or she wasn't chosen. But more often than not, there are several worthy candidates and almost invariably, there is friction or hard feelings from those who don't get recognition. This is especially true at the minor hockey level when addition to the ego of the individual players involved, you have to deal with the ego of the parent. I have tried several approaches to making these selections ... coaches and team staff only, poll of the parents, poll of the players, poll of everyone involved with the team ... but nothing seems to work to my satisfaction. I wish that I had the perfect solution but the best that I can pass along is a sincere good luck!

Despite this potential headache, hopefully the season ends with some sincere handshakes and best wishes for the future. For most minor hockey coaches it is time to put your feet up for a while. Preparations for next year can usually wait a couple of months. Sometimes at the AAA level and certainly at the Junior level and beyond there is some scouting, some recruiting, perhaps a draft to prepare for ... then the planning starts for next season. Some organizations schedule evaluation camps to bring in and look at potential future prospects.

Although this time of year seems to be somewhat anti-climactic and after a long season, it is tempting to just go through the motions, I would suggest that it is when organizations might have their best chance to evaluate and talk to future players. It will pay great dividends if a well planned, systematic approach is used and it has been my observation that the strong organizations in a league do it much better than the weaker ones. As with player evaluation, it is much more effective if more people are involved. A strong scouting staff that has established an effective network is invaluable. Regular communication and meetings ensure that good prospects are detected and stay on the radar screen.

From the player's point of view, the off-season can be an exciting time. Setting a training plan is important and at the junior level and beyond, teams have staff in place to advise and coordinate. At the minor hockey level, there are many professional trainers available these days and more and more athletes are opting to use them. This is also a good time of year to work on power skating and development of other skills.

Choosing a team to try out for in the following season is another issue. At the minor hockey level movement is limited and players tend to stay with one organization. In other jurisdictions there are strong high school hockey programs and again there is continuity from one season to the next. Upon entering junior hockey, however, there are some decisions to be made. Major Junior leagues hold a draft of players and at the elite level, players will be selected. These individuals will be required to go to the team that selects them but they can still select Junior A (sometimes referred to as Tier 2 Junior) as an option.

Why would they do that? Well, there are scholarships available in the U.S. through the National Collegiate Athletic Association (NCAA) that provide players with full tuition for a four year University or College degree. When a player opts to play Major Junior, they receive benefits including paid tuition and a monthly cash allowance and because of that they are considered professionals. As professionals, they become ineligible for

NCAA scholarships. Some players may prefer to play Junior A in order to maintain eligibility for those scholarships. Another benefit is that Junior A leagues tend to require less travel because they encompass a smaller geographic area and so for younger players who are finishing high school, it may be a better option.

What is the best decision? Well, everyone is in a different situation but as a parent, I think that the best advice I was ever given was to have my son play at the highest level that he was capable of. In North America, that would be Major Junior hockey. It is the best caliber of hockey, they provide the young players with much more in terms of equipment and all around training, and they have a very solid educational program. For each season played, they offer players a year of paid tuition at the educational institution of their choice. The down side, of course, is that to play in the league you give up scholarship eligibility so it is important for players to weigh options and make the decision that is best for them. On the other hand, scholarship is only one factor that comes into play when making a decision. Playing junior hockey in any league is exciting and hopefully will be a stepping stone to many more hockey experiences.

Of course not all players have the luxury of deciding between junior hockey options. It is great to have many teams vying for your services but of course there will be many who would be happy with just one possibility. My advice to young players is that if a junior team hasn't contacted you, contact one of them! There are many who would be happy to have a look at you. It may seem that if you don't get drafted or you don't get a camp invitation that you don't have options but when you think about it, scouting is really an imperfect science. At best, scouts will get out and watch a team play a handful of games during a season. With so many players on each team, the chances of them getting a complete picture of any one player is very remote. Usually it is one thing that catches the eye and that may lead to a second look and eventually some interest but of all the great things that get noticed there are probably hundreds of others that don't. There are many good examples of players being discovered at many different stages of their hockey careers ... so it is always worth a try.

My son Sean played some hockey with a young man by the name of Matt Frattin. He was a good player but wasn't taken in the major junior draft and had only mild interest from a couple of Junior A teams. When he was finished playing midget hockey, he wasn't sure if he wanted the commitment of elite hockey any more and was talking about maybe playing for a Junior B team. After some deliberation, he decided to give Junior A hockey a try and after making the team it wasn't long before things just took off for him. By the end of the season he was in the top five of league scoring, had a full scholarship to the University of North Dakota and in the NHL draft was taken by the Toronto Maple Leafs in the third round! That is how quickly things can change.

Billy Moores, presently an assistant coach with the Edmonton Oilers but prior to that the successor of Clare Drake as head coach of the University of Alberta Golden Bears, once told me a great story about Cory Cross. This was a young man who had never played at an elite level and had dabbled in a bit of Junior B hockey before deciding to attend the University of Alberta. Cory was a student in a physical education class that Billy was teaching. When the class took to the ice to play some hockey, Billy was impressed with Cory's tenacity and saw some potential in his set of skills. An invitation to try out for the Golden Bears led to Cory finding a spot on the team. Not only did he go on to play very well for the University team over the next few years, upon graduation he went on to have a successful career in the National Hockey League.

Of course there are all sorts of opportunities to play hockey other than at the highest level. My son Mark wasn't excited about the junior options that were available for him in Canada and after doing some research we found an opportunity for him to play in Sweden. A couple of his friends found an opportunity in a totally different part of the world and had some fun playing semi-pro hockey in Australia. In Canada we have some excellent senior hockey teams and there are numerous men's (and women's) teams available for players at any level.

It saddens me to see Atom players who give up playing hockey because they don't make the tier one team in their area. It saddens me to see fifteen year olds who feel like they no longer have any chance of playing pro hockey because they don't get drafted by a major junior team. It saddens me to see players who weren't quite able to catch on with a Junior A team decide to give up or half heartedly slug away with a Junior B team because they feel that all is now lost. As coaches, I think that it is so important for us to ensure that these youngsters don't give up on their dreams. Recognizing that today is just one point in time and understanding that things can change drastically tomorrow is an important message to get across. For those who aren't able to get there we need to make sure that players never lose their love of the game. There are all sorts of opportunities to play … just for the fun of it!!

Eventually everyone stops playing hockey. Some try briefly and then decide to never lace up a pair of skates again. For others it is a lifelong passion. My Dad, for example, played well into his seventies. As is the case in many other sports, the game has a lot to offer participants in terms of enjoyment and wellness … both physical and mental. Like other team sports it provides players with the experience and satisfaction of working together with others. For our family, hockey was a lifestyle. It took up a lot of time and was, at times, a financial hardship. Nonetheless, as each season passes, I have observed the development of some impressive character traits in my sons … traits that will be very helpful as they walk the path of life. And for each of them, their participation in the game of hockey was an important contributing factor.

So the loose ends of the post season are tied up and as a coach you can finally call it a wrap. There is just one more thing to remember, and this is very important … enjoy your off-season! Coaching, although rewarding, is a very stressful activity. You need time to unwind and recharge your batteries for next season. There may be some seminars or conferences that you want to attend. I always find that these are very energizing. It's great to hear the presentation of new ideas and I find that the networking opportunities are very helpful. But make sure you find time to put your feet up! I find that my most enjoyable seasons are those that are preceded by a good, long rest.

I sincerely hope that you have enjoyed reading "The Season." My objective was to take you through planning considerations that a hockey coach faces while working through a season from start to finish. Along the way I hoped to provide some ideas that could be of some benefit and some opinions that may be thought provoking. Some parts of the book may be more applicable to one age or skill level than another but I hope that there is a little something for everyone. Hockey is a great game and having knowledgeable people involved will only serve to make it better. It would be gratifying to think that maybe I have made a small contribution to that. In any case I hope that you will continue to enjoy the game and for those who are embarking on a coaching career I wish you the best of luck in the future!

Legend

——————▷	forward skating
∿∿∿∿∿∿∿	puck carrying
‿‿‿‿‿‿‿	backwards skating
- - - - - - - - - - -	passing
═══▷	shooting
F	forwards
D	defense
G	goalie
C	coach
X O	players
‖	stopping
▲	pylon
●	puck

Glossary of Hockey Terms

Although this is not a comprehensive list of hockey terms, it does provide an explanation of some of the lesser known ones that are discussed in the book.

Back door pass — A pass, in the offensive zone, across the front of the net to a teammate who is positioned off of the far side goal post.

Box formation — A penalty killing formation in the defensive zone. Two forwards are up high in the zone and two defencemen are low in the zone.

Box plus one — A power play formation which resembles a box in the offensive zone. One defenceman and one forward are wide on each side of the ice and the fifth skater is generally in the middle slot area.

Butterfly — Positioning used by a goaltender when making a save. The legs are spread outward and the pads positioned along the ice in an attempt to block low shots.

Chip pass — A pass made when close to the boards. The puck is flicked by the passer's stick, usually off the boards or glass, to an open area where a teammate is able to retrieve it.

Controlled breakout — A breakout formation used primarily when the opponent is using a forecheck known as the trap. The objective is for all players to skate a pattern that will help open up passing possibilities as the team moves up the ice.

Crossovers — A skating tactic involving crossing one leg over the other that is usually used to help a player with lateral movement across the ice.

Cycling — An attack tactic used to create pressure in the offensive zone and tire to get in good position to receive a pass.

Dryland — The name used to describe off-ice training or practice.

Dump — A tactic used to get the puck past defenders and deep into the offensive zone. Often used along with aggressive skating in attempt to regain possession of the puck and attack the opponent's net (dump and chase).

Finish the check — A phrase used to describe the act of body checking an opponent after he or she has shot or passed the puck. It is used as a means of establishing an aggressive game plan.

Five-hole — Refers to the open area between the goaltenders legs and above his or her stick. It is a favourite target for shooters.

Forecheck - Pursuing the opposition team in the defensive or neutral zone in an attempt to foil their attack and gain control of the puck.

Front the puck - A defensive tactic. It occurs in front of the defensive net when the defenceman moves in front of the opposition player to knock down a shot from the point.

Funneling - An offensive tactic. It refers to the process of shooting pucks towards the opponent's net from inside the offensive zone whenever an opportunity presents itself.

Gap - Refers to the distance between the defender who is retreating and the opposition puck carrier who is attacking. "Gap control" refers to the maintenance of the appropriate distance between the two.

Give and go - An offensive tactic. It is the process of passing to a teammate (the give) and then quickly finding open ice to receive a return pass (the go).

Half wall - Refers to the area along the boards about halfway between the blue line and the goal line. It is a location that is often used to set up an offensive play.

High in the zone - Refers to the area up near the blue line in either the offensive or defensive zone.

Lateral crossovers - Rapidly crossing one leg over the other with toes pointing straight ahead. The movement in this case is directly sideways.

Low in the zone - Refers to the area down near the net in either the offensive or defensive zone.

Neutral zone - Refers to the area in the middle of the rink between the offensive and defensive blue lines.

Offensive zone - Refers to the section of the ice surface that stretches from the boards behind the opponent's net to the offensive blue line.

One-time shot - A term describing the act of shooting the puck in one quick motion as a teammate's pass arrives.

Overload - Sending more than the usual number of players to one side of the ice in an attempt to outnumber the opposition. Overloading can be used as either an offensive or defensive tactic.

Over pass - A pass from a defenceman over to his or her partner on the other side of the ice. It is also known as a "D to D" pass.

Penalty killing - Required to prevent the opposition from scoring when your team has received a penalty and has a manpower disadvantage.

Pivot	- The act of placing a skate, positioning the body and changing the direction of skating. It can be a forward to backward pivot or a backward to forward pivot.
Point	- The area just inside the offensive blue line. Often in this area an offensive defencemen will initiate a shot towards the opponent's net.
Power play	- Arises when a team has a manpower advantage due to a penalty against the opposition.
Power skating	- A term widely used to describe the exercises and drills designed specifically to improve skating ability.
Regroup	- Occurs when the attacking team retreats and moves the puck back towards its own goal. The objective is to give your players time to establish good positioning prior to another attack on the opposition.
Reverse	- An evasive tactic in the defensive zone. A defenceman who is skating with the puck while being pursued by a checker bounces a puck off of the boards in the opposite direction. This will allow a teammate to skate in and retrieve the puck.
Rim the puck	- Occurs when a player shoots or passes the puck along the rink boards using the contour of the boards to establish direction.
Rolling the lines	- A phrase used by coaches to describe the action of sending one line out after the other without interrupting the sequence. It is only possible at certain times of the game because there is often interruption of the flow due to penalties or for strategic reasons.
Saucer pass	- A pass from one player to another that flies over the top of an obstacle … usually a stick. Ideally the puck will spin like a saucer and land flat on the ice surface.
Screening	- The act of using the body to block the vision of a defender. Most often used by the offensive team in front of the opponent's goaltender.
Sealing	Also known as "pinning." It refers to the act of taking away an opponent's ability to move with the puck along the boards.
Scrimmage	- An informal game that usually takes place during a team practice.
Shinny	- An informal, unstructured game of hockey
Shorten the bench	- A phrase used to describe a coach's strategic decision to reduce the number of players used in a game situation.

Slot	- Refers to the area directly in front of the net. The "low" slot is very near the net while the "high" slot is up near the blue line.
Spot pass	- A pass that is made to a specific spot on the ice rather than directly to a teammate.
Spread	- A power play formation which resembles a box in the offensive zone. One defenceman and one forward are wide on each side of the ice and the fifth skater is generally on the half wall.
Soft dump	- A dump-in that is light enough to nestle into a defensive corner instead of rebounding hard off of the end boards. It is a tactic that makes puck retrieval by the opponent much more difficult.
Staggering	- The act of offsetting a defence pairing so that the support player is across and slightly back from the puck carrier. This makes it more difficult for an opponent to intercept passes across the ice from one defenceman to another.
Stay-at-home	- A term used to describe defencemen who have a tendency to stay back and maintain a strong position defensively rather than getting too involved in the team offence.
Stretch man	- Describes a player who is positioned up the ice to provide a long passing option for a team that is breaking out of their zone.
Strong side	- Refers to the side of the ice that the puck is on.
Support	- The act of providing assistance to a teammate.
Swinging	- An offensive tactic. Skating back towards his or her goal, the player flares out to one side or another and then turns up ice. The purpose is to create speed and a passing option to facilitate the movement of the puck up the ice.
Tipping	- The act of getting a stick on a puck that has been shot in an attempt to change its direction prior to reaching the goal.
Tracking	- Pursuit of the opposition's players as they attack your zone with the puck. Also known as "backchecking."
Trap	- A passive forechecking system where all five players are on the defensive side of the puck. The objective is to have the other team come to you and then create a turnover farther up the ice.
Transition	- Occurs when you lose the puck and have to switch from offence to defence or, conversely, when you obtain the puck from an opponent and have to change from defence to offence.
Turn up	- A quick pass from the defenceman to the forward on the

strong side of the puck.

Umbrella	- A power play formation where one defenceman is positioned just inside the offensive blue line in the centre of the ice. He or she is supported by his defence partner at the top of one face-off circle and a forward at the top of the other. The two other forwards are positioned close to the front of the opponent's net.
Weak side	- Refers to the side of the ice that is opposite to the one that the puck is on.
Wall	- A slang term used by hockey coaches to refer to the boards of the hockey rink.
Wheeling	- A term used to describe a defenceman's act of carrying the puck up the ice.

Reading List

I have had the pleasure of reading most of these books. The others have been recommended by coaching colleagues. Thanks in particular to Barry Medori and Rick Swann for their contributions. Reading a new book usually gives me a bunch of new ideas. Hopefully some of these will inspire you!

Technical

Hockey Canada Skills Development	Hockey Canada Manual
The Hockey Drill Book	Dave Chambers
The Incredible Hockey Drill Book	Dave Chambers
Complete Hockey Instruction	Dave Chambers
Hockey Play Book: Teaching Hockey Systems	Michael A. Smith
The Hockey Coaches Manual: A Guide To Drills, Skills and Conditioning	Michael A. Smith
Hockey Drill Book	Michael A. Smith
Laura Stamm's Power Skating	Laura Stamm
Hockey Goaltending	Brian Daccord
Complete Conditioning for Ice Hockey	Peter Twist
The Hockey Goalie's Handbook	Jim Corsi, John Hannon
Coaching Youth Hockey: A BaffledParent's Guide	Bruce Driver, Clare Wharton
Hockey for Dummies	John Davidson, John Steinbreder
Coaching Hockey for Dummies	Don MacAdam
Hockey Drills for Scoring	Newell Brown, Vern Stenlund, K. Vern Stenlund
Hockey Drills for Passing and Receiving	George Gwozdecky, Vern Stenlund, K. Vern Stenlund
Hockey Goaltending	Joe Bertagna
The Bertagna Hockey Goaltending Series	Joe Bertagna
40 of the Best - Canadian National Team Drill Manual – Volume 1	Tom Renney, Mike Johnston
Shots on Goal: Goalies are Players Too	Leo MacDonald

General Hockey

Simply the Best – Insights and Strategies from Great Hockey Coaches	Mike Johnston, Ryan Walter
Simply the Best – Players on Performance	Mike Johnston, Ryan Walter
The Game	Ken Dryden
The Home Game	Ken Dryden, Roy MacGregor
Hockey Tough	Saul Miller
Off the Bench & into the game	Ryan Walter
The 7 am Practice	R. MacGregor

The Home Team	R. MacGregor
In the Crease	Dick Irvin
Grace Under Fire	L. Scanlon
Ice Time	Scott Russell
Champions in Courage	Pat LaFontaine
Of Ice and Men	Bruce Dowbiggin
Coaching, Leadership, Motivation Human Potential	Cal Botterill, Tom Patrick
Flight of the Buffalo	James Belasco, Ralph Stayel
No Ordinary Moments	Dan Millman
The Little Book of Coaching	Ken Blanchard, Don Shula
Leadership and the One Minute Manager	Ken Blanchard
The Double Goal Coach	Jim Thompson
The Inside Edge	Peter Jensen
The Art of Team Coaching	Jim Hinkson
What it takes to be Number 1:Leadership Lessons from Vince Lombardi Senior	Vince Lombardi Junior
No Excuses	Kyle Maynard
Skiing Zen: Searching for the Spirituality of Sport	Rick Phipps
Thinking Body, Dancing Mind	Lynch & Huang
The Way of the Champion	Lynch & Huang
Bird Watching	Jackie MacMullan
Rogers World	Wayne Scanlan
Everyone's a Coach	Blanchard & Shula
True Blue	Dick Weiss
The Complete Player	Saul Miller
In Pursuit of Excellence	Terry Orlick
Joe Torres Ground Rules for Winners	Joe Torre & Dreher
Sacred Hoops	Phil Jackson & Delehanty
More Than a Game	Phil Jackson & C Rosen
Playing for Keeps (Michael Jordan)	D Halberstam
The Monk Who Sold his Ferrari	Sharma
The Saint, the Surfer & the CEO	Sharma
Leadership Wisdom	Sharma
Who Will Cry when I Die	Sharma
Tuesdays With Morrie	Mitch Albom
Who Moved my Cheese	S Johnson
Game Plans for Success	R. Didinger
Great Job Coach	JH Salmela

What it Takes to be #1 (Lombardi on Leadership)	Vince Lombardi Jr
Russell Rules	Bill Russell & Falkner
Finding the Champion Within	Bruce Jenner & Seal
Breakaway	C Wilkins
After the Applause	C Wilkins
Lance Armstrong Its not about the Bike	Armstrong & Jenkins
Lance Armstrong Every Second Counts	Armstrong & Jenkins
Competitive Fire	M Clarkson
Crossing the Line	L. Robinson
Unguarded	Lenny Wilkins & T. Pluto
Coach	Andrew Blauner
The Ultimate Athlete	George Leonard
Raise the Roof	Pat Summitt & Sally Jenkins
Primal Leadership	Daniel Goleman

Biography

Champions	Kevin Lowe, Stan Fischler
Gretzky: An Autobiography	Wayne Gretzky, Rick Reilly
A Life in Hockey: Scotty Bowman	Douglas Hunter
When Pride Still Mattered: A Life of Vince Lombardi	David Maraniss
Wooden	John Wooden and Steve Jamieson
John Wooden, an American Treasure	Steve Bisheff
Knight	Bobby Knight
Clare Drake: The Coaches Coach	Derek Drager
Searching for Bobby Orr	Stephen Brunt
America's Coach: Life Lessons and Wisdom for Gold Medal Success (Herb Brooks)	Ross Bernstein
Grapes: A Vintage View of Hockey	Don Cherry, Stan Fischler
Messier	Jeff Z. Klein
Gordie Howe	Gordie Howe, Frank Condron
Glenn Hall	Tom Adrahtas

Motivational Sports Movies

Coaches are always looking for good sports films to motivate the team. Here is a list of ones that I have enjoyed.

1. Remembering the Titans – Denzel Washington
2. Miracle – Kurt Russell
3. Hoosiers – Gene Hackman
4. Rudy – Sean Astin
5. Radio – Cuba Gooding Jr.
6. Friday Night Lights – Billy Bob Thornton
7. Major League – Tom Berenger
8. Bull Durham – Kevin Costner
9. Field of Dreams – Kevin Costner
10. The Rookie – Dennis Quaid
11. He Got Game – Denzel Washington
12. NHL The Ultimate Gretzky – Documentary
13. Rocky – Sylvester Stallone
14. Coach Carter – Samuel L. Jackson
15. Chariots of Fire – Nicholas Farrell
16. The Longest Yard – Burt Reynolds
17. Slap Shot – Paul Newman
18. The Greatest Game Ever Played – James Paxton
19. Any Given Sunday – Al Pacino
20. Mystery, Alaska – Hank Azaria
21. Glory Road – Josh Lucas
22. Without Limits – Billy Crudup
23. Cool Runnings – Leon
24. The Replacements – James Black
25. Breaking Away – Dennis Christopher
26. Ali – Will Smith
27. A League of Their Own – Tom Hanks
28. Hoop Dreams – William Gates
29. Victory – Sylvester Stallone
30. Bend It Like Beckham – Keira Knightley
31. The Natural – Robert Redford
32. Seabiscuit – Toby McGuire
33. The Pride of the Yankees – Gary Cooper
34. Glory Road – Josh Lucas
35. Invincible – Mark Wahlberg
36. Bobby Jones, Stroke of Genius – James Caviezel
37. Million Dollar Baby – Clint Eastwood
38. Raging Bull – Frank Adonis
39. We Are Marshall – Matthew McConaghy
40. The Hurricane – Denzel Washington
41. All the Right Moves – Tom Cruise
42. Eight Men Out – John Cusack
43. The Legend of Bagger Vance – Will Smith
44. Tin Cup – Kevin Costner
45. The Rocket, the legend of Rocket Richard – Roy Dupuis
46. The Peaceful Warrior – Nick Nolte
47. The Bad News Bears – Walter Matthau
48. The Mighty Ducks – Emilio Estevez
49. Bang the Drum Slowly – Robert De Niro
50. The Express – Rob Brown